No More Hurt

By *Pastor Rhonda Spencer*

Testimony of "No More Hurt"

"Learning about all the true spiritual repercussions of 'the spirit of offense' and how it diminishes my walk with God and His power in my life ~ **changed everything for me!** It was truly my 'fly in the ointment', poisoning whatever endeavors I pursued in God's name. Even watching my mouth, which was a huge one for me, wasn't enough. I was getting frustrated at trying to do so many things right, serving God and disciplining myself to be immersed in His Word ~ yet, still, I seemed to be progressing at a snail's pace.

Even if you do good works and are not 'saying' crappy things about people ~ if you're 'THINKING' them, as I continually was, it is just as spiritually toxic! No wonder I felt like I hadn't arrived and that my connection to God was lukewarm, at best.

I had dealt with a lot of betrayal in my life and, sadly, my first big helpings of that were from my mother. I spent years estranged from family.

In my walk with God, I made great effort to achieve true forgiveness. I asked for God's help to enter authentic forgiveness and He surely honored my request in miraculous fashion and cleared my heart of all the hurts I suffered.

Through Pastor Rhonda's teachings I have studied the spirit of 'offense'. Recently I got my first true test. I had a very close relationship with my brother's wife. We had both weathered great storms and were tremendous support to one another throughout. Well, she went through something huge and heart breaking, and much to my confusion, chose everyone (it seemed) to lean on or confide in but me. My knee jerk reaction was to say, 'Hey what did I do to lose your trust? I've been such a faithful, loyal friend.'

I quickly caught myself. I said, 'She's hurting, confused, in fight or flight mode. I CHOOSE TO NOT MAKE THIS ABOUT ME. I choose to pray for her and not take offense. My conscience is clear, and this is really not about me.' I chose not to be offended. Not only did it preserve our relationship, it saved me from endless toxic thoughts, hurt, sadness and most importantly 'disconnection from God' and the miracles I'm believing in Him for! **Stepping out of the trap of offense in my life CHANGED my life, dramatically!** Humans are broken and act mean. Even the ones we love and trust the most. We will get hurt. We must forgive. But we can choose not to fertilize that hurt and let it drag out and poison our thoughts. That choice will have us walking more fully with God.

Now it is like a muscle I exercise everyday! Since there are so many opportunities in a day to be offended, excitingly enough, there are an equal amount of opportunities to shut down the spirit of offense! And when you do that, God rushes to flood you with His presence! What better reward for choosing a vital principle in His Kingdom over what the world encourages us to think."

-*Susan Murphy, NY*

Other Resources by
Pastor Rhonda Spencer

Available at:
www.RhondaJSpencer.com

No More Hurt and No More Hurt Workbook are printed
by CreateSpace (an Amazon.com company) and are
available at Amazon.com and other retail outlets

No More Hurt

Preface

It is God's desire that His sons and daughters live an abundant life, not a life of hurt. John 10:10 says, "'The thief does not come except to steal, and to kill, and to destroy. I have come that they may have life, and that they may have it more abundantly.'"

Let me start by praying for you right now.
"Father God, I know this pain is so very real. I pray that You will wrap Your loving arms around them and let Your love just penetrate their heart, their mind and their spirit. Keep them from the damage of offense and hurt. Help them to let go and to be healed of this pain. Lord, we pray for the person that this hurt has come from, heal their hurting heart and pains that have caused this hurt to continue to cycle.

Father, I thank you that they are safe and secure in You. I pray that nothing will be able to hurt them ever again and that they will be restored, renewed and made whole. In Jesus' Name I pray these things. Amen"

Nothing, <u>no thing</u> can by any means hurt you.

You have been equipped and authorized to have nothing ever hurt you. Luke 10:19 says, "'Behold, I give you the authority over all the power of the enemy, and nothing shall by any means hurt you.'"

If God has given me the power and authority that nothing can hurt me, I determine the level of my hurt, not my circumstances; not what I was born into and not what anyone else says or does. What I am experiencing is a result of the seeds I have sown. No one, no thing, other than myself, determines the harvest I will reap. Galatians 6:7-9 says, "Whatever a man sows, that shall he also reap."

BUT, John 16:33 says, "In this world you will have trouble."
There are so many opportunities for us to be offended and hurt. How can we achieve this freedom from hurt?

Throughout our lives, we experience hurt, brokenness, rejection, insecurity, fear, loneliness, weakness, bitterness, resentfulness, anger, and jealousy. **This is not how God created us to be.** He came that we would have abundant life, yet somehow we move into this place; and how did we even get here?

Hurt stems from a root of fear; fear of rejection, fear of failure, fear of not being good enough. Whatever the fear is, hurt is based in fear; but knowing God's perfect love will expel all fear. 1 John 4:18 says, "Perfect love expels all fear, for fear has torment, and he that fears has not been made perfect in love." When you can realize how much God loves you unconditionally, that He is for you and not against you, that He has your best in mind at all time; it will take away all fear. You can know that you are safe and secure. People hurt us and reject us, but Jesus never has and never will.

Let me preface this by telling you that I am an expert, by life experience, on the topic of hurt.

If you have been in this world any amount of time you have experienced hurt - most likely more than once - and sometimes to extreme levels. I have lived a life of many hurts. I was abused as a child; my safety and security lost. The hurt of death when a friend was killed in an accident. The hurt of rejection from my father when he walked out on us when I was 16 years old with my mother's best friend. The hurt of abandonment I felt when my father told me he had a new family now and I would just have to deal with it. I lost a baby while my husband was out of town. I had to scoop up the little body and take it and myself to the hospital. My father was murdered and it is still an unsolved case today. One of my good friends was murdered, leaving children behind. After relocating our family to a different state for a job, we were told we were a transitional casualty and the position had been given to someone else. My children have been harmed. We had family killed in an auto accident by a drunk driver. My closest friends have walked out on me, not once but several different times, and several different friends. People that I have done the most for have turned and spoken evil of me. I have been stolen from. My mother (my biggest supporter and helper) died suddenly from an unexpected kidney failure. These are just a few, and I could go on and on. You probably can, too, regarding your own hurts.

So, just in case you think I have just lived a charmed life and that is how I can say **nothing** can hurt you, you can now throw that thought out.

How can I say that you can live with no more hurt?

Here is my journey.
For many years I was a hurt person who, in turn, was hurting others around me.

After a while the hurt was piling up, hurt upon hurt. I cried out to God, begging Him not to let all this hurt change me, not to let it harden me and cause me to become bitter. He heard my prayers, and as I studied His Word, I began to learn how to have no more hurt.

I had to learn my value and my worth and where they come from. It is not easy to do because many times we have our value and worth tied up in other people, our careers, our children, or our skills. As long as that was where my worth was, when, not if, those hurtful things came along, my world was devastated. But what I have learned is that nothing in this world can affect the inside of me, who I am and who I choose to be. I have learned my worth and value do not come from anything in this world. This joy, this peace, this love that I have; this world did not give them to me and the world cannot take them away. Those people that have hurt me, they are not the ones that gave me my joy so they cannot touch my joy. That only happens if I choose to allow it.

Why would you let the person hurting you determine your value, your worth, your hurt level? They do not have your best interests in mind. They are not even considering you at all.

Let me remind you today that when you accept Jesus into your life, you become a **"new creation"**. <u>The old is gone and all things are made new.</u> The hurting person you used to be is not who you are today (or should not be). When you accept Jesus as Lord and Savior over your life, He is just that, **your Savior**. He saves you from the old you. No financial status or social status you hold can change the heart, hurts, or your mind, but Jesus can. He makes all things new.

2 Corinthians 5:17 "Therefore if any man be in Christ, he is a new creation: old things are passed away; behold, all things are become new."

The way to stop hurt is to renew the way we think, and that will take practice and exercise. As you enter the chapters that follow you will be confronted with challenges I pray you will choose to practice and exercise so that you will experience life with no more hurt.

Chapter 1

Worth & Value

Our worth and value comes from what we are giving the highest platform to or the loudest voice to. God desires that He be first and the highest. He wants to be the voice that we listen to and trust in. He desires this because He created us and He knows what will be best for us. He always has your best interests in mind.

When we are hurt, we are choosing to value what someone else said or did to us over what God says about us.

I know this can be a challenge when those people and hurts are so real and in our faces. God knows if we hold those things above Him that we can be hurt, discouraged, depressed and destroyed.

Your value does not decrease because of something someone else says or does to you.

A $100 bill does not lose its value just because **"life happens."** It still has the same value and is still equally accepted. I can do just about any damage to a $100 bill and if I gave it to you, you would accept it and readily spend it. You never lose value in God's Kingdom. You are of immeasurable worth to Him. All of your brokenness, pain and hurt does not devalue you at all. Life changes and shifts and our positions and roles change too. If our value is in whatever that season is shifting from, we can be left feeling worthless; but we are still the valuable person that we have always been. It just feels and looks different now.

We put more faith in hurt and the people who hurt us, than in God and His Word. 1 John 4:4 says, "Greater is he that is in you than he that is in the world. God's Word should be what we hold above everything else. In Ephesians 6 it says we have been given an armor to protect us. When we hold the Word above every other word spoken, we are putting our armor on. It says faith is our shield. When we put our trust and confidence in God and His Word, that is our shield of faith. We actually have a shield held up in front of us that will block "every fiery dart." Yes, I said every fiery dart. Nothing will be able to hurt you.

The Word of God will quench hurt, just as a shield blocks anything launched at it.

The Amplified Version says in Ephesians 6:16 "Lift up over all the [covering] shield of saving faith, upon which you can quench all the flaming missiles of the wicked [one].
Quench means something coming toward you, and it is destroyed/defeated before it can get to you. So the shield of faith will quench the missile before it can get to you.

If hurt is in your life,
get the Word of God and get it into you.

Keep the Word of God there and any time words of hurt come to you, you will have the shield up. Someone can cuss you out and say all manner of stuff against you, but if you have the shield up you will be able to say "Bless you" because you will remember that the Word of God says **bless those who curse you**. When the shield is not up, the world will drag you into hurt and the words launched at you will penetrate your heart.

So if you are going to get out of hurt, you must keep the shield of faith up.

You cannot be a successful Christian without the Word
of God because without it, when the dart comes,
you will have no shield to hold up.

Your Shield=Faith in the Word of God.
Study to show yourself approved. Hunger for the Word of God. Find out what the Word says about the hurt that you have.

When our trust and confidence is not put in God, but in others and what they say or do, we have no shield. With no shield you are exposed to every dart that comes. You will be wounded and could even be destroyed.

We must keep our armor on and that comes from being in the Word of God. We learn to trust someone the more we spend time with them. It is the same with God, spend time in His Word and your trust and confidence in Him will grow. The more you learn about God, the more incredible He is and the easier to increase your faith and trust in such a perfect, powerful and loving God.

Likewise, the more time we spend dwelling on what hurt happened, the more the hurt will grow.

It is vital that you are in the Word often, getting strength, value, purpose and wisdom. When you do this no thing will be able to touch you, you will be shielded from hurt, pain and offenses. The only way you can get hurt is when you put down your faith in the Word of God and lift up what someone else has said. You have to hold up the shield. Put it down and you are exposed and people will hurt you. You are giving them more power than you are giving the Word of God and what God says about you. You are either going to hold the shield of faith up in your mind or you are going to hold up what someone says about you in your mind. What someone says about you can **hurt** you. If the Word of God is being upheld, then there is **no way** for the words of hurt to get through. Those words will be quenched. If you put the Word of God down, <u>**you are exposing yourself**</u> to all that other stuff. For example, the Bible says that you are the more than a conquerer, versus a person who might say that you are stupid and weak. The only reason that hurts is because you do not have the shield of faith up that says, *I am more than a conquerer*. If you put the shield down, that stuff comes in. Then you believe the lies and "as a man thinketh so is he."
So what does this practically look like? When hurt happens, grab your Bible and read and read and sometimes read a little more until you feel armored up. The best part of first finding your worth and value from God is that it is like a probiotic, working beforehand.

4

You can actually get to the place that no matter how great the hurt or offense that comes is, it does not even effect you (beyond the initial shock, of course).

Keep the **Word** on in your life. <u>You would not try to walk around in a dark house, so do not keep walking around in a dark life.</u> "Thy Word is a lamp unto my feet and a light unto my path." I do not know how to live, behave, act or react properly without the Word of God.
When you are in the Word it is like having solid rock under your feet. You do not have to feel like you are in sinking sand. Without the Word, it can feel like the world is crashing down around you and you are left overwhelmed and hurting.

The more we get God's Word into our minds and hearts, the more peace that reigns in our lives. Things that used to offend us are no longer an issue. God's Word has become the deciding force for our personal identity, not what others say or think about us. We have to allow His Word - also called a "two-edged sword" - to work as a scalpel within our attitudes and motives, cutting off all patterns of thinking that differ from what Scripture declares. This is how we become conformed into His image. In John 16:1 Jesus states it this way, "'These things have I spoken unto you, that ye should not be offended.'" (KJV)

An example of practicing God's Word on a constant basis would be to carefully study the Scriptures. Then *whenever you have an opportunity to be offended, make a decision to respond according to the instruction of these Scriptures*, rather than how you might have reacted in the past. Over time, you will find maturity happening in your life as you continue to put these Scriptures into practice.

You will also find that you are able to distinguish good and evil in your actions and reactions with others. ***You will know when you are reacting in a way that is contrary to God's way when you encounter an offense***, and you will know when you have responded in a good way.

God's Word acts like positive pressure within our lives, resisting any other pressure coming against us. A balloon will stay blown up as long as the pressure inside the balloon is greater than the pressure pushing against it from the outside. If the outside pressure becomes greater than the pressure within, the balloon will pop. In the same way, God's Word is to become a positive force within us. As long as it's pressure is greater than any stress we are experiencing from without, we will not cave in. With life, we do not just get to fail the test and it is done. We get to take the test over and over again until we pass. Failing the hurt test over and over just compounds the pain we have to endure. We need to learn how to have no more hurt so we can get on to living in the peace that God has for us. He did not create us to live hurting.

One of the enemy's strongest weapons is suggestion, and when he uses that weapon, cast down every thought and keep your mind on the Word.

If the enemy's thoughts can get in your head, then the emotions necessary to support that thought will show up. When you apply the Word of God it will pull down the wicked thought.

All of hell is ready to test you! Make sure you have been exercising and practicing. Hold your faith in the Word up above everything else. It is your shield.

3 John 1:2 says, "Beloved, I pray that you may prosper in all things and be in health, just as your soul prospers."

We are as healthy as our souls are prospering.

Our health is directly linked to the prospering of our souls. The Word, the Word, the Word! Watch the Word transform your life & health.

Pitch your tent in hope: "Therefore my heart rejoiced and my tongue exulted exceedingly; moreover, my flesh also will dwell in hope [will encamp, pitch it's tent, and dwell in hope in anticipation of the resurrection]. You have made known to me the ways of life; You will enrapture me [diffusing my soul with joy] with and in Your presence" (Acts 2:26, 28 AMP).

The Word of God is our hope,
let's pitch our tent in hope.

We need to get our nose in the Word and dwell there! Do not put it down.

Where are you pitching your tent? Hurt, anger, fear, rejection? Or hope, peace, love, joy? **It is our choice!** I choose to camp (dwell) in peace, love and joy. A favorite old song of mine says, "This joy that I have, the world did not give it to me, the world did not give it and the world cannot take it away." This is what separates joy from the false senses of happiness, pleasure and thrills.

7

When you have joy, the devil can throw everything he has against you and you just keep on pushing—not because you are that strong, but because God is bigger than anything that life can do to you.

Philippians 4:7-9 says, "And God's peace [shall be yours, that tranquil state of a soul assured of it's salvation through Christ, and so <u>fearing nothing</u> from God and being content with it's earthly lot of whatever sort that is, that peace] which transcends all understanding shall *__garrison__* and mount guard over your hearts and minds in Christ Jesus. Brethren, whatever is true, whatever is worthy of reverence and is honorable and seemly, whatever is just, whatever is pure, whatever is lovely and lovable, whatever is kind and winsome and gracious, if there is any virtue and excellence, if there is anything worthy of praise, think on and weigh and take account of these things [fix your minds on them]. Practice what you have learned and received and heard and seen in me, and model your way of living on it, and the God of peace (of untroubled, undisturbed well-being) will be with you."

__gar·ri·son__ *[gar-uh-suhn]* *noun   dictionary.com*
1. a body of troops stationed in a fortified place.
2. the place where such troops are stationed.
3. any military post, especially a permanent one.

Your worth and your value do not come from this world and nothing in this world can take it away.

To God you are of immeasurable value and there is no one "more special" than you.

8

THE MOST POWERFUL VOICE
IN MY LIFE IS
GOD'S WORD.
HE DIED FOR ME, HE SAVED ME,
HE RANSOMED ME.
YOU'VE DONE NONE
OF THOSE THINGS FOR ME,
SO PLEASE DON'T MIND IF
I AM NOT MOVED OR DEFINED
BY YOUR WORDS.

Joshua 1:8 (NIV)
"Keep this Book of the Law always on your lips; meditate on it day and night, so that you may be careful to do everything written in it. Then you will be prosperous and successful."

Psalm 119:165(KJV)
"Great peace have they which love thy law: and nothing shall offend them."

Psalms 43:5 (NKJV)
"Why are you cast down, O my soul? And why are you disquieted within me? Hope in God; For I shall yet praise Him, The help of my countenance and my God."

John 16:33 (AMP)
"I have told you these things, so that in Me you may have [perfect] peace and confidence. In the world you have tribulation and trials and distress and frustration; but be of good cheer [take courage; be confident, certain, undaunted]! For I have overcome the world. [I have deprived it of power to harm you and have conquered it for you.]"

Romans 8:28 (VOICE)
"We are confident that God is able to orchestrate everything to work toward something good and beautiful when we love Him and accept His invitation to live according to His plan." He knew we would have troubles and knew life would not be perfectly... no matter what could or does go wrong, it is no surprise to Him - He promised each of us that He will always bring us through and out on top!

Psalm 46:1-5, 10, 11 (AMP)
"GOD IS our Refuge and Strength [mighty and impenetrable to temptation], a very present and well-proved help in trouble. Therefore we will not fear, though the earth should change and though the mountains be shaken into the midst of the seas, Selah [pause, and calmly think of that]! There is a river whose streams shall make glad the city of God, the holy place of the tabernacles of the Most High. God is in the midst of her, she shall not be moved; God will help her right early [at

the dawn of the morning]. Let be and be still, and know (recognize and understand) that I am God. The God of Jacob is our Refuge (our High Tower and Stronghold). Selah [pause, and calmly think of that]!"

Habakkuk 3:19 (AMPC)
"The Lord God is my Strength, my personal bravery, and my invincible army; He makes my feet like hinds' feet and will make me to walk [not to stand still in terror, but to walk] and make [spiritual] progress upon my high places [of trouble, suffering, or responsibility]!"

When we put our trust/confidence in flesh as opposed to God:

Proverbs 25:19 (KJV)
"Confidence in an unfaithful man in time of trouble is like a broken tooth or a foot out of joint."

Psalm 118:8 (AMP)
"It is better to trust and take refuge in the Lord than to put confidence in man."
1 Timothy 1:19 (AMP)
"Holding fast to faith (that leaning of the entire human personality on God in absolute trust and confidence) and having a good (clear) conscience. By rejecting and thrusting from them [their conscience], some individuals have made shipwreck of their faith."

Proverbs 29:25 (AMP)
"The fear of man brings a snare, but whoever leans on, trusts in, and puts his confidence in the Lord is safe and set on high."

When we put our trust/confidence in God, these are the promised results:

Psalm 56:3 (AMP)
"When I am afraid, I will have confidence in and put my trust and reliance in You."

Psalm 57:1 (AMP)
"Be merciful and gracious to me, O God, be merciful and gracious to me, for my soul takes refuge and finds shelter and confidence in You; yes, in the shadow of Your wings will I take refuge and be confident until calamities and destructive storms are passed."

Psalm 62:8 (AMP)
"Trust in, lean on, rely on, and have confidence in Him at all times, you people; pour out your hearts before Him. God is a refuge for us (a fortress and a high tower). Selah [pause, and calmly think of that]!"

Proverbs 3:26 (AMP)
"For the Lord shall be your confidence, firm and strong, and shall keep your foot from being caught [in a trap or some hidden danger]."

Proverbs 14:26 (AMP)
"In the reverent and worshipful fear of the Lord there is strong confidence, and His children shall always have a place of refuge."

Jeremiah 17:7 (AMP)
"[Most] blessed is the man who believes in, trusts in, and relies on the Lord, and whose hope and confidence the Lord is."

Mark 5:34 (AMP)
"And He said to her, 'Daughter, your faith (your trust and confidence in Me, springing from faith in God) has restored you to health. Go in (into) peace and be continually healed and freed from your [distressing bodily] disease.'"

Luke 5:20 (AMP)
"And when He saw [their confidence in Him, springing from] their faith, He said, 'Man, your sins are forgiven you!'"

Luke 8:48 (AMP)
"And He said to her, 'Daughter, your faith (your confidence and trust in Me) has made you well! Go (enter) into peace (untroubled, undisturbed well-being).'"

Luke 17:6 (AMP)
"And the Lord answered, 'If you had faith (trust and confidence in God) even [so small] like a grain of mustard seed, you could say to this mulberry tree, "Be pulled up by the roots, and be planted in the sea," and it would obey you.'"

Hebrews 3:6 (AMP)
"But Christ (the Messiah) was faithful over His [own Father's] house as a Son [and Master of it]. And it is we who are [now members] of this house, if we hold fast and firm to the end our joyful and exultant confidence and sense of triumph in our hope [in Christ]."

Hebrews 3:14 (AMP)
"For we have become fellows with Christ (the Messiah) and share in all He has for us, if only we hold our first newborn confidence and original assured expectation [in virtue of which we are believers] firm and unshaken to the end."

Hebrews 6:11-13 (AMP)
"But we do [strongly and earnestly] desire for each of you to show the same diligence and sincerity [all the way through] in realizing and enjoying the full assurance and development of [your] hope until the end, in order that you may not grow disinterested and become [spiritual] sluggards, but imitators, behaving as do those who through faith (by their leaning of the entire personality on God in Christ in absolute trust and confidence in His power, wisdom, and goodness) and by practice of patient endurance and waiting are [now] inheriting the promises.
For when God made [His] promise to Abraham, He swore by Himself, since He had no one greater by whom to swear."

Hebrews 10:35 (AMP)
"Do not, therefore, fling away your fearless confidence, for it carries a great and glorious compensation of reward."

2 Peter 3:14 (AMP)
"So, beloved, since you are expecting these things, be eager to be found by Him [at His coming] without spot or blemish and at peace [in serene confidence, free from fears and agitating passions and moral conflicts]."

1 John 2:28 (AMP)
"And now, little children, abide (live, remain permanently) in Him, so that when He is made visible, we may have and enjoy perfect confidence (boldness, assurance) and not be ashamed and shrink from Him at His coming."

11

1 Samuel 2:2 (AMP)
"There is none holy like the Lord, there is none besides You; there is no Rock like our God."

2 Samuel 22:1-3 (AMP)
"My God, my Rock, in Him will I take refuge; my Shield and the Horn of my salvation; my Stronghold and my Refuge, my Savior."

Psalm 27:5 (AMP)
"For in the day of trouble He will hide me in His shelter; in the secret place of His tabernacle will He hide me; He will set me high upon a rock."

Psalm 40:2 (AMP)
"He drew me up out of a horrible pit [a pit of tumult and of destruction], out of the miry clay (froth and slime), and set my feet upon a rock, steadying my steps and establishing my goings."

Psalm 62:2 & 7 (AMP)
"He only is my Rock and my Salvation, my Defense and my Fortress, I shall not be greatly moved. With God rests my salvation and my glory; He is my Rock of unyielding strength and impenetrable hardness, and my refuge is in God!"

Matthew 7:24-25 (AMP)
"'So everyone who hears these words of Mine and acts upon them [obeying them] will be like a sensible (prudent, practical, wise) man who built his house upon the rock. And the rain fell and the floods came and the winds blew and beat against that house; yet it did not fall, because it had been founded on the rock.'"

2 Corinthians 12:9 (AMP paraphrased)
"God's grace (your power for a living) it is enough for you.

Ecclesiastes 9:4 (AMP paraphrased)
"As long as you are in the land of the living there is hope."

James 3:2 (WBT paraphrased)
"If a man can control his tongue he can control his whole body.

1 Timothy 1:5-7 (AMPC)
"Whereas the object and purpose of our instruction and charge is love, which springs from a pure heart and a good (clear) conscience and sincere (unfeigned) faith. But certain individuals have missed the mark on this very matter [and] have wandered away into vain arguments and discussions and purposeless talk."

Chapter 2

Handling Rejection

Some days I have to coach myself moment by moment. Just today I stood in front of my mirror and said, "Rhonda, you are valuable and immeasurably important to Daddy, keep going." I do not have people in my life who tell me that with their words or actions and you may not either. I know your mind will tell you that you are the only one that feels like this or gets treated like this, but it is just not true. You are not alone. We are all basically the same and have the same needs, and no human can fill them. We must let people off the hook of our need to be accepted and appreciated. Doing so will help us to experience no more hurt.

If we do things for the affirmation and acceptance of others, it is just a matter of time before we become hurt.

Not that people are out to get us; it is just that everyone, even those who love us - will at some point not meet our expectations of acceptance. They may not be able to drop everything to make sure we feel the way we want to feel, as first and most important. Do what you do for God and not for men. We should do everything we do as if we were doing it for God, because we are.

Colossians 3:23-24 (NLT) says, "Work willingly at whatever you do, as though you were working for the Lord rather than for people. Remember that the Lord will give you an inheritance as your reward, and that the Master you are serving is Christ."

> ***When we do what we do for God,***
> ***it is never wasted time or effort.***

It is not just a temporary reward of fleeting acceptance or affirmation, it becomes everlasting when we do it for God.

When someone hurts you or does not treat you as you expect them to for all that you have done for them, you can simply say, "That is okay. I did it to please Father God, anyway." You may have to remind yourself several times of this when you start to feel the sting of hurt. There is nothing wasted when you have done it for Christ. There will be a reward.

When you shift your way of thinking from putting your worth and acceptance in how people react and respond to you, to doing it for God, then you know there is always a reward.

You can become willing to do whatever you need to do to be accepted, even if it means you have to turn the control of your life over to someone else for them to use you.

When you are driven by the fear of rejection, you are not in control. If your main goal in life is to be approved and accepted by other people all the time, you are setting yourself up to be used and hurt. Your actions are saying you do not mind being used in order to be accepted.

You are willing to give that steering wheel over to someone else just to use you. Sometimes women are willing to do this; turn something so private as your own bodies over to somebody else, doing everything you cannot to make them mad, even when you know they are not good for you in the first place. Women put up with abuse just to not make them mad.

Parents are afraid to discipline their children for fear of them not liking them or rejecting them. You are called to be their parent <u>not their friend</u>. The fear of being rejected will stop us from stepping into that role.

So if you crave acceptance and fear rejection, the object of your affection will have the power to manipulate and hurt you. If you are so hungry to be accepted, you become beelined toward being hurt. Have some love for yourself. Face your fear of rejection. If you do not, you are setting yourself up to be exploited. Your actions are saying, "I am so afraid, I will do anything to be accepted." <u>The devil is written all over this</u>.

The devil wants to get you so afraid of being rejected, that you are willing to do anything to be accepted.

There is one person who will <u>never</u> reject you.

Ephesians 1:5-6 says, "Having predestined us to adoption as sons by Jesus Christ to Himself, according to the good

15

pleasure of His will, to the praise of the glory of His grace, by which He made us <u>accepted</u> in the Beloved."

Romans 8:39 says, "Neither Height nor depth, nor any other created thing, shall be able to separate us from the love of God which is in Christ Jesus our Lord."

Galatians 4:4-6 says, "But when the fullness of the time had come, God sent forth His Son, born of a woman, born under the law, to redeem those who were under the law, that we might receive the adoption as sons. And because you are sons, God has sent forth the Spirit of His Son into your hearts, crying out, 'Abba, Father!'"

1 Thessalonians 5:9-11 says, "For God did not appoint us to wrath, but to obtain salvation through our Lord Jesus Christ, who died for us, that whether we wake or sleep, we should live together with Him. Therefore comfort each other and edify one another, just as you also are doing."

No, you are **not** willing to do anything to be accepted. No, you will **not** do anything to avoid rejection. No, you are **not** willing to do anything to be married. You do **not** let someone come up to you and say they will marry you but you have to be willing to have sex with them first. You will say, "It took me a long time to feel good about myself and I am not about to let one night tear down everything I have worked for in my life. I am not giving it up, and do not call me anymore because I do not have time for this yo-yo game. My feelings are important to me. You can find someone else who is willing to do anything for you but I am not like that. I am somebody!"

You lose a sense of self worth as you fear rejection. If you fear rejection, you become like a chameleon. You develop the ability to change your color depending on your surroundings. You act one way with your family, another way with people at work and another way with people at church.

Have you ever noticed how people change depending on who they are around? The fear of rejection will cause you to compromise and to conform. All of a sudden, you expose yourself to the point of wanting to be accepted so bad you have lost your self worth.

I remind you, child of God, there is someone that has said, "I will never reject you."

So I am going to trust the One that will never leave me or reject me.

This is how you fight feelings of rejection. Let's talk about how to get free from the fear of rejection. The first step is to get born again (accept and acknowledge Jesus as your Lord and Savior) and realize you are a new creature.

John 6:37-38 says, "'All that the Father gives Me will come to Me, and the one who comes to Me I will by no means cast out. For I have come down from heaven, not to do My own will, but the will of Him who sent Me.'"

I do not need to feel rejected when I get born again, I am accepted.

Proverbs 18:24 says, "A man who has friends must

himself be friendly, But there is a friend who sticks closer than a brother."

I do not need to compromise my standards in order to be accepted. If God will accept me, He can bring the right people around my life, and I will not have to compromise and do all kinds of things to be accepted.

2 Corinthians 5:17 says, "You are a new creature, behold all things are become new."

Realize the fear of rejection is a feeling and you need to do everything not to turn your life over to your feelings. You cannot let rejection take charge of your life. You will never go anywhere if you do. The potential for rejection is *everywhere*. You have got to be bold enough to step out and not be afraid of someone telling you no. No <u>cannot</u> be a word to make you feel bad.

No has got to be a word that inspires you to come back better!

Do not allow your life to be ruled by rejection. You are not a reject! You are a new creation in Christ Jesus!

I want people who want me for who I am, not because of what I have got to pretend to be. Besides if you wear too many hats you may get the wrong hat on at the wrong time. If I see you in the market, I do not have to try to figure out what hat to put on if I am just me. **There is nobody else like you!** Be the best you that **you** can be for Him.

Our diversity makes life interesting and fun. Find out

what it means to be the righteousness of God, and to be in right standing with God. You are kings and priests with Him, joint heirs of Jesus. You are royalty not a mere sinner, a new creation. Knowing His perfect Love for us casts out all fear. Greater is He that is in you than he that is in the world.

It is awful hard to walk around feeling rejected when you know who is inside of you, who is for you, who is holding your hand and when you know who has accepted you.

If I am good enough that God accepted me,
then I am good enough for anybody.

If anyone rejects you it is their loss. Maybe you had an absent father who was never a part of your life or that just abandoned you at some point. **You did not do anything.** I feel sorry for him, because he missed the opportunity to see you grow into a strong man or woman of God. He missed out. You have a Daddy, Abba Father in heaven, who accepted you. He is the best Father; a good and perfect Father.

You cannot keep living in those past rejections. Let them go. If you are saved, you have got somebody. You have got Jesus, and He is all you will ever need.

Rejection can hurt, so you must forgive those who have rejected you. They do not know what they have missed out on. Stop being the victim in everyone's drama and in your own. You cannot control what others think or say about you, so stop worrying about it. You do not really need to be accepted by others, but what you need to know is that you are accepted by God. Do not be co-dependent;

having to have someone to feel good about yourself. God gave us a standard of how to feel **(the Word of God)**. Line yourself up with that standard and you will not need anyone else to determine how you feel.

> *"I do not need anyone to be accepted as long as I am accepted by God."*

Rejection is a real feeling but we have to learn to stand up to it. We have God in our lives; a God who has committed to never reject us. When you walk like that, other people look at you and they see the confidence and they want that. They want to be like that. Be happy all by yourself and be bold to go out and show the confidence of a God who has a covenant with you that He will not reject you.

If you want to get free from this fear of rejection, find others that hurt worse than you do. You will be amazed to find out what happens in your life when you seek out someone who has gone through it worse than you have. When you start ministering to them, that is the quickest way to get ministry to come back to you. "Give, and you will receive. Your gift will return to you in full - pressed down, shaken together to make room for more, running over, and poured into your lap. The amount you give will determine the amount you get back" (Luke 6:38 NLT). When you get so busy extending what you have to someone else, healing takes place in your own life.

To be used as an instrument of God to be a blessing in someone else's life is the ultimate fulfillment. There is nothing like being a blessing!

You are blessed to be a blessing.

Then you just do not have time to be rejected when you are more concerned about what you can do for other people. Philippians 2:3 says, "Consider others more important than yourselves."

When our expectations of others are not met, it can leave us feeling rejected even though that may not be the case at all. We expect that everyone will always be faithful, we expect that they will do their best by us, we expect them to treat us fair and kind. People are human and will fail us, sometimes without even meaning to or trying to. When we place "God standard" expectations on people, we set ourselves up for hurt and we put them in an unrealistic place. People are not God; they are human and fall short. When we do this, it is like we put God in human standards and then we end up viewing Him as one who will hurt us too. God will never fail you but people will, even those close to us. When our expectations are not met we are left feeling hurt. Give people room to be human, expect that they will be human and make mistakes, just like you do and have done to others. We hold others to a standard we do not even keep ourselves. Have you ever talked negative about someone? Have you ever been sharp with anyone? Have you ever been so focused or busy that you did not even say hello to someone? Have you ever forgotten and not showed up to something you said you would? I am sure I have disappointed people before, even though I did not try to. Expect that others will do the same and let them off the hook of unrealistic perfection. Maybe they are having a bad day or going through something themselves. You never know what a person is going through, so give

21

allowance for humanness in your expectations and it will keep you from disappointment and hurt. Remind yourself that God is perfect but people are not and neither are you.

Fear has torment, and the hurt of rejection is based in fear. So if you are wallowing in rejection, torment will show up.

Do not give Satan that access into your life!

It will lead you into low self-esteem, then you will be angry with everyone, and depression will set in. All because you did not understand the importance of taking authority over the fear of rejection. You are special and important to God. You are the apple of His eye. He will never leave you nor forsake you. If we can get a reality of God in our lives, rejection will never have power.

Just because the fear of rejection led you astray into hurt, fear and torment, it does not mean that the covenant God has for you has to remain broken. A decision can cause you to enter back into that covenant, just as a decision caused you to break it.

Every time you sense rejection coming your way, just say right out loud,

"Jesus, You are all I need and I know You are right here with me, You will never leave me or forsake me."

"I am accepted and I do not need to do anything to be accepted by those who do not have my best in mind. I am safe and secure. I know I am perfectly loved by God, therefore I have no fear."

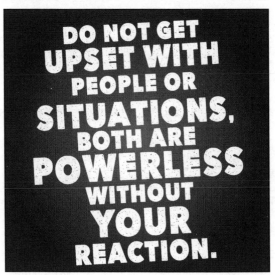

DO NOT GET UPSET WITH PEOPLE OR SITUATIONS, BOTH ARE POWERLESS WITHOUT YOUR REACTION.

Romans 11:1 (NASB)
"I say then, God has not rejected His people, has He? May it never be!"

John 6:37 (ESV)
"whoever comes to me I will never cast out."

Acts 10:34-35 (NASB)
"Opening his mouth, Peter said: 'I most certainly understand now that **God is not one to show partiality**, but in every nation the man who fears Him and does what is right is welcome to Him.'"

Ephesians 1:5 (NLT)
"God decided in advance to adopt us into his own family by bringing us to himself through Jesus Christ. This is what he wanted to do, and it gave him great pleasure."

Psalm 27:10 (ESV)
"For my father and my mother have forsaken me, but the Lord will take me in."

Philippians 3:3-14 (Amp)
"For we [Christians] are the true circumcision, who worship God in spirit and by the Spirit of God and exult and glory and pride ourselves in Jesus Christ, and put no confidence or dependence [on what we are] in the flesh and on outward privileges and physical advantages and external appearances—Though for myself I have [at least grounds] to rely on the flesh. If any other man considers that he has or seems to have reason to rely on the flesh and his physical and outward advantages, I have still more! Circumcised when I was eight days old, of the race of Israel, of the tribe of Benjamin, a Hebrew [and the son] of Hebrews; as to the observance of the Law I was of [the party of] the Pharisees, As to my zeal, I was a persecutor of the church, and by the Law's standard of righteousness (supposed justice, uprightness, and right standing with God) I was proven to be blameless and no fault was found with me. But whatever former things I had that might have been gains to

me, I have come to consider as [one combined] loss for Christ's sake. Yes, furthermore, I count everything as loss compared to the possession of the priceless privilege (the overwhelming preciousness, the surpassing worth, and supreme advantage) of knowing Christ Jesus my Lord and of progressively becoming more deeply and intimately acquainted with Him [of perceiving and recognizing and understanding Him more fully and clearly]. For His sake I have lost everything and consider it all to be mere rubbish (refuse, dregs), in order that I may win (gain) Christ (the Anointed One), And that I may [actually] be found and known as in Him, not having any [self-achieved] righteousness that can be called my own, based on my obedience to the Law's demands (ritualistic uprightness and supposed right standing with God thus acquired), but possessing that [genuine righteousness] which comes through faith in Christ (the Anointed One), the [truly] right standing with God, which comes from God by [saving] faith. [For my determined purpose is] that I may know Him [that I may progressively become more deeply and intimately acquainted with Him, perceiving and recognizing and understanding the wonders of His Person more strongly and more clearly], and that I may in that same way come to know the power outflowing from His resurrection [which it exerts over believers], and that I may so share His sufferings as to be continually transformed [in spirit into His likeness even] to His death, [in the hope] That if possible I may attain to the [spiritual and moral]

resurrection [that lifts me] out from among the dead [even while in the body]. Not that I have now attained [this ideal], or have already been made perfect, but I press on to lay hold of (grasp) and make my own, that for which Christ Jesus (the Messiah) has laid hold of me and made me His own. I do not consider, brethren, that I have captured and made it my own [yet]; but one thing I do [it is my one aspiration]: forgetting what lies behind and straining forward to what lies ahead, I press on toward the goal to win the [supreme and heavenly] prize to which God in Christ Jesus is calling us upward."

Romans 8:15 (ESV)
"You have received the Spirit of adoption as sons, by whom we cry, "Abba! Father!"

Romans 8:31 (ESV)
"What then shall we say to these things? If God is for us, who can be against us?"

Romans 8:38-39 (KJV)
"For I am persuaded, that neither death, nor life, nor angels, nor principalities, nor powers, nor things present, nor things to come, Nor height, nor depth, nor any other creature, shall be able to separate us from the love of God, which is in Christ Jesus our Lord."

John 1:12 (ESV)
"But to all who did receive him, who believed in his name, he gave the right to become children of God."

Chapter 3

Hurting People Hurt People

Part 1
(Being Understanding of Others &
Believing The Best in Every Situation)

This is the single most powerful revelation on my journey to live with no more hurt. Happy people do not go around hurting people; hurting people hurt people. I have taught my children this from the time they were young. They would come home from the bus upset because someone said something mean, or from school because a person did something hurtful, or from the park because a person was being a bully. I would explain to feel compassion for them because something bad must have been going on in their life that caused them to do those things. They were not happy people and they must be hurting, because only hurting people hurt people. If you can learn this principle and really apply it, it will save you a world of future hurt and will help you let go of some of the hurt you are holding on to right now. Strive to understand; do not fight to your own death to be understood.

Believe me, I know, this is way easier said than done. I had about 6-7 major hurts and betrayals by people I loved and cared for before this moved from head knowledge to heart knowledge. You can know that it is only hurting people that hurt people and still allow it to hurt you. I did for years. I had studied how to not hurt, I had taught it to my children. I had even preached it. When someone hurts us, it is natural to want to protect ourselves, and so we villainize that person. They are just bad or evil. This is just who they are. We make them the bad guy in order to make ourselves feel better about it. This may make us temporarily feel better but it does nothing for the hurt feeling it caused. We are left still hurting.

My years of study, teaching, preaching about and villainizing people that hurt people came to a screeching halt one day. One of my closest friends that I had known from school hurt me (well now I would say she was hurting). I had helped her back on her feet, gave her a job and really loved and believed in her, and she hurt me. See how we make it all about us? I had a problem because this person was one of the best people I knew. She was caring, loving and joyful. I was unable to make her into a bad person or villainize her because I **knew** she was not.

It was this time around the mountain (taking the test over) that I was realizing it is not all about me, it is not about me at all.

She must have been really hurting. Bad things were going on in her home with her husband, scary things involving her children. She had stepped out on her husband and began a relationship with another man, just looking for safety and security. She pushed me away and would not talk to me, she even began to say bad things about me. When this all began to happen I did not know what was

26

going on inside her, and I still do not know for sure to this day. All I saw was what I was feeling, and what it was doing to me. I was stuck though. I could not make her out to be a villain, because she was the sweetest person I knew. It was in this season that all my teaching, preaching and training about hurt kicked in. She was not a bad person just out to be mean. She must have been really hurting and in pain to do this. My poor, precious, sweet friend was hurting so bad she began to hurt the people around her. I only had love and compassion for this person who was genuinely doing hurtful things, and my initial hurt never grew into offense or bitterness but only love and compassion. I had no more hurt.

Here is another scenario: A man went out to a local restaurant. The service he got was slow and below the standards expected. The man went on the Internet and did a review and gave it only mid-range rating and told of the poor service that day. Now, outraged, the restaurant owner comes out slinging mud and how disappointed he was at the review. Everyone in this scenario was left hurting and feeling bad with bitter feelings. How different it could have been if each person realized that hurting people hurt people. The slow service could have been the server or the cook having a rough day. Maybe their car broke down on the way to work and they had to have it towed and walked the rest of the way in; or they got a call that their mother was rushed to the hospital. By realizing everything is not about you, and assuming the best first, you will save yourselves from hurt. This explosive situation could have been stopped before it got to hurt. How about if the restaurant owner would have thought, *Wow, I know this guy. He must be having a bad day. Maybe his dog just died or he woke up not feeling good today, or maybe he was in a lot of pain.* What if his response was compassion, knowing only hurting people hurt people? What if he had reached out and said, "Man I am really sorry that happened today. Is everything okay with you? Why don't you come in tomorrow and your lunch is on me?" How differently this would have ended without the hurt. How about if someone on social media, rather than throwing wood on the fire, would have been a peacemaker instead and cared enough to reach out and see if everyone was okay? Matthew 5:9 says, "Blessed are the peacemakers."

When I had my light bulb moment with this, I was able to let go of so many hurts. I could now see that yes, it was truly only hurting people that hurt people. I could see that even in myself. When I am hurting I tend to hurt people too, where I normally would not act or react like that. Knowing this helps break the cycle of hurt, because when I am hurting I can be aware and strive not to cause hurt. It is called making allowance for other people.

Colossians 3:13 says,
"Make allowance for each other's faults,
and forgive anyone who offends you.
Remember, the Lord forgave you,
so you must forgive others."

If you hold onto hurt it will only cause more hurt and you will be a part of the cycle that we have way too much of already - hurt people hurting people. At times, we all have been a part of this cycle whether we are the hurt or the hurting.

Other people's ugliness cannot effect us unless we allow

28

it to. <u>It does not matter how nasty or mean another person is, that is of no affect to you.</u> One of the easiest ways to get hurt to subside quickly is to think of it like a fire. If you put no wood on the fire, it goes out. If you put no words, complaining or justifying on an offense, it will stop raging. I have learned to not argue my point, justify my actions or try to explain my side. All this does is keep the fire going and the hurt gets deeper. Proverbs 26:20 (ASV) says, "For lack of wood the fire goeth out; And where there is no whisperer, contention ceaseth."

It is so easy to think of how everyone else should be living, acting and behaving. We have no control over that, but we do have control over us.

It is called "mind your own business". I strive to simply look in the mirror of my life and mind myself. What can I do to bring peace to this situation? How can I respond and not add fuel to the fire? I have plenty of work to do on me without worrying about the speck in another's eye. Choose to look at yourself and not the other person's actions. How am I reacting to this hurt? How am I behaving? What do I look like right now? The way this cycle stops is by not being hurt and you do that by minding you, being understanding of others and realizing that person is probably hurting in someway. If you allow hurt in, you will only propel that hurt onto others. Then, how long will you hold on to the hurt and pain that will continue, like a snow ball, to build more and more? Hurt people, hurt people. Do not villainize them; empathize with them! Expect the ungodly to be ungodly; they have and know no other way. I feel sorry for anyone going through this life who does not have God in it.

Are you trusting God as your Lord, or them?

Who are you trusting in right in the middle of the storm? I want my trust to be in the I am, that I am.

We must watch our reaction to hurt to break the cycle of hurting people hurt people. A lie we fall for is, "It is more important to protect the way I feel right now (my reaction), than to protect my future." If someone calls you something or does something mean or that you do not like at work, instead of understanding hurting people hurt people, you want to quit your job. 20-30 years ago, when people hurt people at work, they didn't walk off the job. They did not have the luxury to sit back and be prideful and we certainly do not have that luxury today. But we still do it with no thought of our future, just of our immediate feelings.

You cannot build anything on the unstable foundation of hurt. You have to let it go and release those people. You can get stuck in a go nowhere lifestyle for years. I know grown, older adults who have built nothing with life and still only have a broken foundation of hurt. The power to have no more hurt is completely in your hands.

Romans 12:21 (ESV)
"Do not be overcome by evil, but overcome evil with good."

2 Timothy 2:23 (NKJV)
"But avoid foolish and ignorant disputes, knowing that they generate strife."

Proverbs 15:18 (NKJV)
"A wrathful man stirs up strife, But he who is slow to anger allays contention."

Proverbs 18:2 (NLT)
"Fools have no interest in understanding; they only want to air their own opinions."

Romans 14:19 (KJV)
"Let us therefore follow after the things which make for peace, and things wherewith one may edify another."

Proverbs 13:10 (NKJV)
"By pride comes nothing but strife…"

Chapter 3

Hurting People Hurt People

<u>Part 2</u>
(Our Part in the Cycle of Hurting People Hurt People)

In Part 1 of this chapter, we learned to try to understand that the reason others hurt us is because they are hurting. We can see the personal freedom and power that comes from believing the best in every situation. In Part 2 we will see how to understand ourselves and how we participate in the cycle of hurting people hurt people.

Sometimes hurt comes from not understanding why God did not do something you asked.

Job 15:11-13 says, "'And you have been offered comforting words from God. Isn't this enough? Your emotions are out of control, making you look fierce; that's why you attack God with everything you say.'"

You can get offended with God and become hurt but He is the only one that can get you out of your mess. <u>If you get offended at God you are leaving yourself stranded.</u>

I cannot move a mountain or hang the stars. Job made

the mistake of dethroning God and God responded in Job chapter 38, <u>"Were you there when I formed the world, did you hang the stars, do you tell the ocean to end and go no farther than the shore?"</u> *ooooooooh*

I want HIM to be my God. **<u>You cannot spiritually afford to be offended with God.</u>** This leaves you having to be your own god. Quit crowning yourself as your god. Let God be your God. He will work things out that you canNOt work out.

The All Powerful can do it way better than you can.

See, God does not do only what you ask! The Bible says God will do more than what you ask and not just more, but exceedingly, abundantly more than you can ask. Watch this - nothing has even been asked yet. It says more than you **ask** or **think**.
"Now to Him who is able to do exceedingly abundantly above all that we ask or think, according to the power that works in us (What does *His* power do in us? It works.), to Him be glory in the church by Christ Jesus to all generations, forever and ever. Amen" (Ephesians 3:20-21 NKJV). I am so convinced that maybe certain things have not been working out in your life because you have been trying it your own way.

It is easy to say He is God when everything is good. In the middle of the storm *who do I say that He is*? Do I *still* trust Him? Is He still my Healer, my Protector, my Refuge? "He is the same Yesterday, Today and Forever" (Hebrews 13:8).

He is the help in the time of trouble until you try to help

yourself. One way we try to help ourselves is with worry.

It is a sin to worry; it is a slap in God's face.

Worry is negative meditation. If you think negative thoughts, those negative emotions will show up to support those thoughts and will leave you hurt. The more we practice making God our help, the more the results are marvelous. You will be more powerful as you practice this. You are sealing up the access the enemy used to have to get into your life. Determine that God is going to be your God.

If you get offended by not understanding God, you are going to be stuck in the cycle of hurt people hurting people, acting mean and fierce.
A big revelation for me in not being offended by God was my realization that I only see a very small piece of the picture and God sees the whole thing. He knows how it is going to play out on the eternal spectrum. It is as if there is a beautiful painting but all you see is a small brown square of it. You are trying to figure out what the picture is of, but you cannot even possibly begin to; it is just a tiny brown square. "My thoughts are nothing like your thoughts," says the LORD. "And my ways are far beyond anything you could imagine. For just as the heavens are higher than the earth, so my ways are higher than your ways and my thoughts higher than your thoughts." (Isaiah 55:8-9 NLT).

Sometimes we just have to trust that we will not and cannot understand all things, and that is okay.

"Being confident of this very thing, that he which hath

begun a good work in you will perform it until the day of Jesus Christ" (Philippians 1:6 KJV).

"And we know that God causes everything to work together for the good of those who love God" (Romans 8:28 NLT).

"So let's not get tired of doing what is good. At just the right time we will reap a harvest of blessing **if we don't give up**." (Galatians 6:9 NLT)

Don't be offended with God and "give up". Why does that sound like a better option to us? This will only cut God out, keep Him from working in our lives and leave us stranded.

You keep doing what is good. Even if the situation never changes, you will be blessed and you will keep the power of God working in your life.

Don't fall for the lie that "giving up" is a better option.

I do not think like God, His thoughts and ways are higher than mine. I remember as a child I would try to get my brain to understand eternity, that there was no beginning ever, God just always was. It almost hurt my brain to strain so hard to understand something I was incapable of understanding with my human mind. God's ways are much like that, we sometimes cannot wrap our brains around them and that is okay because He is God. We do not have to understand everything. Some things we will not be able to understand because we can only see the little brown square no matter how hard we try. It is in these times we have to trust. We have to hold up our

34

shield of faith so that the fiery darts of the enemy will not be able to take us out. We need to pitch our tents in hope in God. We need to know that we are safe and secure in Him and that we stand on the solid Rock.

Sometimes God gets blamed for things that are not from Him. God is good all the time and the devil is bad. I am convinced that God has had to say, "that was not Me" while not being heard because we are so bent to blame Him. Everything good comes from God.

"Whatever is good and perfect comes down to us from God our Father. He never changes or casts a shifting shadow" (James 1:17 NLT).

Everything bad comes from the enemy of your soul, the devil. "'The thief does not come except to steal, and to kill, and to destroy. I have come that they may have life, and that they may have it more abundantly'" (John 10:10 NLT).

Stop blaming God.

The only two limits God put on Himself are: He will never go against His Word and He will never go against a person's free will. We get mad at God, but it is not God, it is a person's own choice. There are some bad and evil people in this world that will do bad and evil things. God does not control that. We want God to control that but that is not what He wanted. In order for us to love and experience genuine love, it has to be of free will choice and not robotic programming. So along with that free will choice comes the ability for people to choose evil. It is never God's desire that one would choose evil. Stop

35

being mad and offended at God. God is always good and everything good comes from Him. If it is bad, <u>place blame where it belongs - on the devil</u> who is the one who steals, kills and destroys.

Sometimes hurt comes when someone we love unexpectedly dies. My mom died very unexpectedly, without signs, symptoms or warning. I begged God to help me. I was numb, like a zombie walking around. I did not care about anything or anyone. I remember standing in church singing (well everyone else was singing, I refused) and the words were "I took back what the enemy stole from me." Those words stung. I could not have back what was taken from me. It made me angry and more hurt than ever to know I could never have my mom back. It was then that I heard the still small voice of the Lord, "That is not what was stolen from you. What was stolen from you was your joy, your love, your peace; and those I can return to you in a moment." Wow! I had been suckered to think what was stolen was my mom, when actually what was stolen was my smile, my joy, my love, my peace; and those things could be returned to me. What had been months of hurt, in a moment was healed and restored. It was like a magic trick; while my eyes were focused over there, my pockets got emptied right before my eyes and I did not even know it. Just like you would snatch back your things upon discovering this, I took back what was stolen from me.

When dealing with the loss of a loved one, it is so hard for our finite minds to comprehend that they are in eternity. If they are in heaven, to them it is like they will see you tomorrow. A lifetime, when you enter eternity, is just as quick as if you blinked your eye. Yes, that is an entire lifetime in comparison to eternity. To them, they will see you in the blink of an eye.

"Nevertheless, do not let this one fact escape you, beloved, that with the Lord one day is as a thousand years and a thousand years as one day." (2 Peter 3:8 AMP)

"For you, a thousand years are as a passing day, as brief as a few night hours." (Psalms 90:4 NLT)

I miss my mom but how could I be upset, she is in a perfect place? No pain, no sorrow and she will see me "tomorrow." I could stay in that hurting, angry, depressed, sulking place but she would never want that for me. She would want me to be filled with love, joy and peace.

So cast off the spirit of heaviness and put on a garment of praise. It is your choice.

Are you letting the enemy distract you all the while he is robbing you?

And how long will you allow this? It is okay to be sad (Jesus wept), but do not remain there too long. You are being robbed of life while your eye is being distracted. Maybe you have a job, a ministry, children or a spouse who need you; you have got to keep living. Death will happen to us all. "Each person is destined once to die" (Hebrews 9:27 NLT).

To live with no more hurt is going to require restraint in your emotions. Hurt IS fear-based. When your feelings are hurt, you begin to pull up your protection devices because you are afraid of what might happen again. My husband, Dr. Micheal Spencer, teaches there is a cycle to love: every time you love, you open yourself up to be vulnerable; every time you become vulnerable, it is inevitable you will get hurt; every time you get hurt, you must choose to forgive and love again. Every time you love, you open yourself up to be vulnerable; every time you become vulnerable, it is inevitable you will get hurt; every time you get hurt, you must choose to forgive and love again. So the cycle of love goes.

Or you can stay a part of the cycle of hurt and say, "I am hurt and I am afraid you are going to hurt me again so now I am cynical, I have hardened my heart. I am going to hurt you before you hurt me. I am going to do all the wrong things to try to resolve my hurt because of the root of fear." When our emotions are attacked negatively, we must not yield to fear, because fear will take us right away from the love of God and faith in God and will drive us headlong into hurt. Perfect love casts out all fear, therefore perfect love will cast out hurt and fear, if you walk in it.

1 John 4:18 says, "There is no fear in love; but perfect love casts out fear…"

> *When we accept that God has nothing but*
> *unconditional love for us*
> *we will be in peace and void of all fear.*

Unconditional love is like meeting someone and knowing nothing about them, with no preconceived notions. It is like meeting them on the "blind auditions" on The Voice TV show; you don't get to see them or know who they are. Anyone who says they are of God has this same love in them.

Love is not a feeling, it is a choice.

1 Corinthians 13:4-8 says, "Love suffers long and is kind; love does not envy; love does not parade itself, is not puffed up; does not behave rudely, does not seek it's own, is not provoked, thinks no evil; does not rejoice in iniquity, but rejoices in the truth; bears all things, believes all things, hopes all things, endures all things. Love never fails. But whether there are prophecies, they will fail; whether there are tongues, they will cease; whether there is knowledge, it will vanish away."

Perfect Love was willing to die for even those rejecting Him. This display of perfect love is the opposite of hurt people hurting people and is the love that is inside of every son and daughter of God. The choice is yours to be a part of the cycle of love or the cycle of hurt.

Deuteronomy 30:19 (NLT)
"Today I have given you the choice between life and death, between blessings and curses. Now I call on heaven and earth to witness the choice you make. Oh, that you would choose life, so that you and your descendants might live!"

Romans 13:10 (NIV)
"Love does no harm to a neighbor."

Ephesians 5:1-2 (ESV)
"Therefore be imitators of God, as beloved children. And walk in love, as Christ loved us and gave himself up for us, a fragrant offering and sacrifice to God."

Ephesians 4:27 (ESV)
"Give no opportunity to the devil."

Matthew 7:12 (NET)
"In everything, treat others as you would want them to treat you."

Chapter 4

I am Not Hurt, Just Offended

"Well, you see, I am not hurt like that, I am just offended by them." I want to call attention to this crafty ploy of the enemy. Many "mature" people cannot be tripped up by the big, obvious things, so the enemy of our soul has used a masterful technique, and it is called offense.

In our minds, we come to church to worship God, to learn, to be equipped, and to grow; but something very different ends up happening. We come into church so busy being offended that ***we do not actually worship God*** or learn or grow, and we cannot even hear from God because we are too busy being offended. We *think* we do because we are present at church each week, but therein is the ploy. The enemy of your soul knows human nature so well, he does not even care if you go to church because he knows he can stop you from worshipping God.

Maybe it is like this:

*Ugh that person is sitting in **my** seat, I sit there every week and everyone knows it.*

I thought Julie was my friend. She just walked right by me and never said "Hi." What did I ever do to her? How rude; and she calls herself a Christian?

That music is just awful! It is so loud; they will never be able to keep people with it screeching like that.

They walk right by me every week and do not even acknowledge that I exist.

They are so two-faced. They act one way in church but I know how they act outside. They are not fooling me, they are such a hypocrite. I am not going there anymore there are too many hypocrites.

Oh my goodness, I cannot believe she wore that to church. This is the house of God. I would never! In whose thinking is that even okay? What a hussy! Really, I cannot even worship in a place where that is okay. Why won't anyone say anything to her?

They are so mean spirited, I do not even want to be around them.

I am not ever going to sit here again. All they do is talk, right out loud. How rude! I cannot even concentrate. As a matter of fact, I cannot sit over there and I definitely cannot sit behind those teens. Actually, I cannot sit anywhere. Those people - all of them - are just so disrespectful. I am just going to find another church where it would be better.

How am I doing so far? Does this sound like some of your self talk during your time of "worship?"

I know, I know, maybe it is just me. You see, we could not receive from God, even though our intention is to come to learn and grow and worship, because we are so busy interrupting what God wants to say by being offended.

It is not the church that is the problem.

We feel dry, empty and so far from God because, week after week, we go through the motions of church but we are *not actually getting to worship, learn or grow*. So, 10 years in, we feel like the church has failed us, and we need to go somewhere else to get fed. That will work for a few weeks until you get back into the same old routine of offense!

I do not mean to step on your toes, but the enemy is in the camp, and I care enough to sound the alarm.

Offense is hurting us.
If you are feeling hurt or angry, you have an offense.

These are just some offenses that are inside the church. How about our work places? Oh, the opportunity for offense is so vast there. It can cause us to quit, lose our jobs, or stay on, be miserable and make everyone else's lives miserable too.

How about driving? The check out line? The bank? The gas station?

Then, *what about our homes*? Our children? *Our spouses*? Offense will sever even these valuable unions established by God. We can give no place to offense in our lives; but it is so stealthy, so we must uncover it.

__Seriously, we just spend all day every day with opportunity for offense.__

Let me show you what offense does. We will start with just the scientific, physical part: *__offense causes hurt and tension__* which can literally cause sickness and disease in our bodies. It is scientifically proven to effect our health.

Even more is what offense does spiritually:

Mark 6:3-5 (NKJV) says, "'Is this not the carpenter, the Son of Mary, and brother of James, Joses, Judas, and Simon? And are not His sisters here with us?' So they were offended at Him. But Jesus said to them, 'A prophet is not without honor except in his own country, among his own relatives, and in his own house.' __Now He could do no mighty work there__, except that He laid His hands on a few sick people and healed them.'"

Did you get that? They were offended and He was not able to do mighty works there. They were unable to experience the power of God.

__Offense stops the power of God from being able to work in our lives!__

Mark 4:16-17 (AMP) says, "'And in the same way the ones sown upon stony ground are those who, when they hear the Word, at once receive and accept and welcome it with joy; And they have no real root in themselves, and so they endure for a little while; then when

43

trouble or persecution arises on account of the Word, they **immediately are offended** (become displeased, indignant, resentful) **and they stumble and fall away.'"**

Matthew 24:10 (AMP) says, "'And then **many will be offended** and repelled and **will begin to distrust and desert [Him Whom they ought to trust and obey] and will stumble and fall away and betray one another and pursue one another with hatred.'"**

The enemy of our soul is on task 24/7 and he does not rest in his job to steal kill and destroy. We must fight the good fight, daily.

We have to get rid of the offenses we already have and make sure at the same time we avoid the every moment opportunity for a new offense to come in.

Ecclesiastes 10:1 (KJV) says, "Dead flies cause the ointment of the apothecary to send forth a stinking savor: so doth a little folly him that is in reputation for wisdom and honor."

1 Corinthians 5:6 (NLT) says, "Don't you realize that this sin is like a little yeast that spreads through the whole batch of dough?"

Offense seems like just a little thing, but this little thing can be so destructive. Offense is a seed that you are sowing into your life and *__you will reap of it's harvest__*.

God spoke to me clearly on this subject. I have been in church pretty much my whole life. I go every Sunday and I thought I was a pretty mature Christian until God shed light on offenses. I was not really worshipping God or mature, and I was so distracted with offense. My brain told me I was all good because I was in church each week, but the reality is I may not have "gone to church" very often at all.

We may think an offense is no big deal. We think: I will just avoid them. I can ignore them. It is just a few people anyway. I do not care about them, they are nothing to me.

Matthew 25:40 (NKJV) says, "And the King will answer and say to them, 'Assuredly, I say to you, inasmuch **as you did it to one of the least of these My brethren**, you did it to Me.'"

Oh, that stings. "As you did it to one of the least of these, **you did it to Me**." Just as we are doing to those we consider so little of, that is actually how we treat Christ, Himself. **What**? That is exactly what God is saying here. Ask yourself, how is it that I treat the person or people that I do not think much of or very highly of? How do you treat those people that offend you? That is how you have treated Christ.

What a powerful revelation this was to me:
I had actually been treating Christ one way all the
while I was thinking I was mature and honoring Him.

1 Corinthians 13:5 (AMP) - God's Love
"It is not conceited (arrogant and inflated with pride); it is not rude (unmannerly) *and* does not act unbecomingly. Love (God's love in us) does not insist on it's own rights *or* it's own way, *for* it is not self-seeking; it is not touchy *or* fretful *or* resentful; it takes no account of the

evil done to it [it pays no attention to a suffered wrong]."

1 John 4:7-8 (NKJV) - Knowing God Through Love
"Beloved, let us love one another, for love is of God; and everyone who loves is born of God and knows God. He who does not love does not know God, for God is love."

When I shared this, I had someone come to me and say: "I did not know the kingdom of God is so difficult and elite, with so many boundaries." My response was: *"it is not, maybe we have just gone so far from what it is supposed to be like."*

It is like cleaning a room or a garage. If you do not do any cleaning, it gets so bad you do not even know where to start. If we maintain it, it does not get out of hand.

Matthew 7:13-14 (NKJV) - The Narrow Way
"'Enter by the narrow gate; for wide is the gate and broad is the way that leads to destruction, and there are many who go in by it. Because narrow is the gate and difficult is the way which leads to life, and there are few who find it.'"

Sometimes the offense we take can be actual condemnation from our accuser, the devil. God's word says: "there is therefore no condemnation to those who are in Christ Jesus" (Romans 8:1). To condemn means to pronounce guilty. The devil would love for you to feel like you have been pronounced guilty; pronounced guilty before God and in the minds of others around you. If you have repented and asked forgiveness, your sin is gone as far as the East is to the West. So you know this is the accuser, because that is condemnation. Do not take up offense over condemnation.

Now conviction on the other hand, is a good thing. That is the Holy Spirit pointing out something you have not repented from that needs to be removed from your life. Sometimes we get offended at God when we feel conviction. Do not get offended with God. He is the only one that can get you out. He is the way to heaven.

Offense may seem so very little; <u>but it stops the power of God from working in your life</u>.

Do not allow ***any*** offense in. I don't know about you, but I cannot afford to be offended. I **need** the power of God in my life working every moment of every day.

What if the offense is valid?

You cannot offend the dead.

It is no longer I who lives, but Christ who lives in me. I have been crucified with Christ.

Galatians 2:20 (NLT)
"My old self has been crucified with Christ. It is no longer I who live, but Christ lives in me."

John 3:30 (KJV)
"He must increase, but I must decrease."

2 Corinthians 5:21 (KJV)
"For God made Christ, who never sinned, to be the offering for our sin, so that we could be made right with

God through Christ."

Matthew 6:14-15 (NIV)
"'For if you forgive men when they sin against you, your heavenly Father will also forgive you. But if you do not forgive men their sins, your Father will not forgive your sins.'"

Luke 6:37 (AMP)
"Acquit, forgive and release (give up resentment, let it drop) and you will be acquitted and forgiven and released."

Acquit means to relieve from a fault or a charge, declare not guilty. See how this is so opposite of the enemy, the devil, and his devices of condemnation and offense.

Colossians 3:13 (NIV)
"Bear with each other and forgive one another if any of you has a grievance against someone. Forgive as the Lord forgave you."

Ephesians 4:31-32 (NIV)
"Get rid of all bitterness, rage and anger, brawling and slander, along with every form of malice. Be kind and compassionate to one another, forgiving each other, just as in Christ God forgave you."

Proverbs 17:9 (CEV)
"You will keep your friends if you forgive them, but you will lose your friends if you keep talking about what they did wrong."

1 Corinthians 13:5 says pay no attention to a suffered

wrong (AMP).

The best response to an offense, even a valid one, comes from Jesus Himself: "When they kept on questioning Him, He straightened up and said to them, *'If any one of you is without sin, let him be the first to throw a stone at her'*" (John 8:7 NIV).

I am not saying this so we can feel beat up. I did not feel that way at all when God had me looking in the mirror. Yes, I felt like a wretch, but I was so grateful that God loved me enough to tell me now and didn't wait until I stand before him unable to do anything about it.
So let's do something about it! It is possible to not live in offense, but how do we do this?

Philippians 1:10 (NKJV) says, "That you may be sincere and without offense till the day of Christ."

HERE'S THE HOPE:

James 5:16 (AMP) says, "**Confess** to one another therefore your faults (your slips, your false steps, **your offenses**, your sins) and pray [also] for one another, **that you may be healed and restored [to a spiritual tone of mind and heart].** The earnest (heartfelt, continued) prayer of a righteous man **makes tremendous power available [dynamic in it's working].**

Do you want tremendous power available to you, dynamic in it's working? *__Then get rid of offenses__.*

None of us wake up in the morning with the thought, "I think I will get offended today." We do not intend for offense to happen. Unfortunately, we also do not take precautions to avoid offense, ***it just happens***.

God's Word is what will keep us from offense. His Word is that two-edged sword that works like a surgeon's scalpel, cutting away anything that is different from what the Word declares.

Psalm 119:165 (KJV) says, "Great peace have they which love thy law: and nothing shall offend them."

This verse has a condition and promise. <u>Great peace and nothing offending</u> is the promise, to those <u>who love thy law (the Word)</u> is the condition.
John 16:1 (KJV) says, "These things have I spoken unto you, that ye should not be offended."

Plan to refuse offense. Whenever you have an opportunity to be offended, make a DECISION to respond according to the love of God (according to the instructions of these scriptures), rather than how you might have reacted in the past.

I know we have had a mirror held up and we have seen the hard truth, but please, <u>do not make any excuses, rationalize or justify</u>.

Strive to not be offended ever; it will keep you in health, in peace, it will keep you from bitterness, from walking away and it will keep the power of God flowing in your lives.

This is exactly what you need for today. It is not too much or too hard. It is too much to stay in offense. It will cost you way too much; including everyone you influence, *even generations to come.*

2 Corinthians 2:11 (NKJV) advises us to be aware of this danger. "Lest Satan should take advantage of us; for we are not ignorant of his devices".

Galatians 2:20 (NLT)
"My old self has been crucified with Christ. It is no longer I who live, but Christ lives in me."

John 3:30 (KJV)
"He must increase, but I must decrease."

2 Chronicles 7:14 (KJV)
"If my people, which are called by my name, shall humble themselves, and pray, and seek my face, and turn from their wicked ways; then will I hear from heaven, and will forgive their sin, and will heal their land."

Galatians 5:13-15, 17, 22, 23, 26 (AMP)
"For you, through love you should serve one another. For the whole Law [concerning human relationships] is complied with in the one precept, You shall love your neighbor as [you do] yourself. But if you bite and devour one another [in partisan strife], be careful that you [and your whole fellowship] are not consumed by one another. For the desires of the flesh are opposed to the [Holy] Spirit, and the [desires of the] Spirit are opposed to the flesh (godless human nature); for these are antagonistic to each other [continually withstanding and in conflict with each other], so that you are not free but are prevented from doing what you desire to do. But the fruit of the [Holy] Spirit [the work which His presence within accomplishes] is love, joy (gladness), peace, patience (an even temper, forbearance), kindness, goodness (benevolence), faithfulness, Gentleness (meekness, humility), self-control (self-restraint, continence). Against such things there is no law [that can bring a charge]. Let us not become vainglorious and self-conceited, and challenging and provoking and irritating to one another, envying and being jealous of one another.

Proverbs 17:9 (CEV)
"You will keep your friends if you forgive them, but you will lose your friends if you keep talking about what they did wrong."

John 8:7 (NIV)
"When they kept on questioning him, he straightened up and said to them, 'If any one of you is without sin, let him be the first to throw a stone at her.'"

Colossians 3:13 (NIV)
"Bear with each other and forgive one another if any of you has a grievance against someone. Forgive as the Lord forgave you."

Ephesians 4:31-32 (NIV)
"Get rid of all bitterness, rage and anger, brawling and slander, along with every form of malice. Be kind and compassionate to one another, forgiving each other, just as in Christ God forgave you."

Proverbs 17:9 (CEV)
"You will keep your friends if you forgive them, but you will lose your friends if you keep talking about what they did wrong."

1 Corinthians 13:5 (AMP)
Says: "pay no attention to a suffered wrong".

2 Corinthians 5:21 (NLT)
"For God made Christ, who never sinned, to be the offering for our sin, so that we could be made right with God through Christ."

Matthew 6:14-15 (NIV)
"For if you forgive men when they sin against you, your heavenly Father will also forgive you. But if you do not forgive men their sins, your Father will not forgive your sins.'"

Luke 6:37 (AMP)
"Acquit, forgive and release (give up resentment, let it drop) and you will b acquitted and forgiven and released."

Chapter 5

People are of Immeasurable Value

Everyone has value and worth and all people are of immeasurable value to God. We need to change the way we see people. We see people through a selfish lens, a measuring lens or sometimes even a competitive lens. Everyone is important and God loves them, even your worst enemy. Gulp! This was a difficult realization for me to grasp. God died for us while we were yet sinners. Yes, even while we were unlovely and still in our sin; and that means anyone who is unlovely and in sin.

We are called to believe the best in every situation and in every person. God's Word teaches us how to hurt no more; we need only to follow it. His ways are higher. Believe the best of everyone.
"Love bears up under anything and everything that comes, is ever ready to believe the best of every person, it's hopes are fadeless under all circumstances, and it endures everything [without weakening]"
(1 Corinthians 13:7 AMP).

Let's take a look at how we are to see others, even our enemies:

"But I say to you who hear: Love your enemies, do good to those who hate you, bless those who curse you, and pray for those who spitefully use you. To him who strikes you on the one cheek, offer the other also. And from him who takes away your cloak, do not withhold your tunic either. Give to everyone who asks of you. And from him who takes away your goods do not ask them back. And just as you want men to do to you, you also do to them likewise. But if you love those who love you, what credit is that to you? For even sinners love those who love them. And if you do good to those who do good to you, what credit is that to you? For even sinners do the same. And if you lend to those from whom you hope to receive back, what credit is that to you? For even sinners lend to sinners to receive as much back. But love your enemies, do good, and lend, hoping for nothing in return; and your reward will be great, and you will be sons of the Most High. For He is kind to the unthankful and evil. Therefore be merciful, just as your Father also is merciful" (Luke 6:27-36 NKJV).

Do not get upset with what is being said, put this book down and stop reading. Remember this is for you, for your peace, your joy and your love. This is so you do not have to hurt anymore. *Keep reading*.

We need to have our mind transformed in how we see people. We need to honor all people.

"Honor all people. Love the brotherhood. Fear God. Honor the king" (I Peter 2:17 NASB).

Every time we speak or interact with someone, anyone, everyone, we should conduct ourselves with humble, meek respect.

The word for *honor* from both the Greek and the Hebrew means to look upon and deal with someone as a valued individual. We have to realize that all people are of immeasurable value to God. We are to give each other respect and honor that is genuine; that comes from transforming our thinking. It must be our desire to honor and please God. It must be our desire to not hurt, or allow anything to hurt us. You say you do not want to have any more hurt, but are your actions saying the same? We honor God by obedience to His Word. So we are honoring God when we choose to honor and respect others - even those with whom we disagree, and those we dislike! This will show our trust of and worship to God. We show our true desire to have no more hurt when we choose to honor all people.

"If you love only those who love you, why should you get credit for that? Even sinners love those who love them! And if you do good only to those who do good to you, why should you get credit? Even sinners do that much!" Luke 6:32-33 (NLT)

Here is another scripture passage that teaches us to value others, even those who hate us:
"At the place where the road passes some sheepfolds, Saul went into a cave to relieve himself. But as it happened, David and his men were hiding farther back in that very cave! 'Now is your opportunity!' David's men whispered to him. 'Today the Lord is telling you, "I will certainly put your enemy into your power, to do

with as you wish.' So David crept forward and cut off a piece of the hem of Saul's robe. He said to his men, 'The Lord forbid that I should do this to my lord the king. I should not attack the Lord's anointed one, for the Lord himself has chosen him.' So David restrained his men and did not let them kill Saul. After Saul had left the cave and gone on his way, David came out and shouted after him, 'My lord the king!' And when Saul looked around, David bowed low before him. Then he shouted to Saul, 'Why do you listen to the people who say I am trying to harm you? This very day you can see with your own eyes it isn't true. For the Lord placed you at my mercy back there in the cave. Some of my men told me to kill you, but I spared you. For I said, "I will never harm the king—he is the Lord's anointed one." Look, my father, at what I have in my hand. It is a piece of the hem of your robe! I cut it off, but I didn't kill you. This proves that I am not trying to harm you and that I have not sinned against you, even though you have been hunting for me to kill me. May the Lord judge between us. Perhaps the Lord will punish you for what you are trying to do to me, but I will never harm you.' When David had finished speaking, Saul called back, 'Is that really you, my son David?' Then he began to cry. And he said to David, 'You are a better man than I am, for you have repaid me good for evil. Yes, you have been amazingly kind to me today, for when the Lord put me in a place where you could have killed me, you didn't do it. Who else would let his enemy get away when he had him in his power? May the Lord reward you well for the kindness you have shown me today. And now I realize that you are surely going to be king, and that the kingdom of Israel will flourish under your rule'" (1 Samuel 24:3-4, 6-12, 16-20 NLT).

And here is the argument that is the icing on the cake for me! "But even Michael, one of the mightiest of the angels, did not dare accuse the devil of blasphemy, but simply said, 'The Lord rebuke you!' This took place when Michael was arguing with the devil about Moses' body" (Jude 1:9 NLT).

Even though the devil is pure evil, Michael would not accuse him. It actually says he did not dare to, this shows such a high level of honor ***not for anything to do with the devil and what he deserved, but it was simply for Michael***. We can choose to be a vessel of honor no matter what or who we are dealing with, much like forgiveness is not so much for the other person ***but it is for ourselves***.

Oh how I desire to be this kind of vessel of honor!

Because Satan is the accuser of the brethren, he goes before God day and night accusing. He loves it when we do his bidding. Many times we the "saints" accuse so much we actually are giving the enemy leverage. "Then I heard a loud voice shouting across the heavens, 'It has come at last— For the accuser of our brothers and sisters has been thrown down— the one who accuses them before our God day and night'" (Revelation 12:10 NLT).

> ***Our fight is never against flesh and blood,***
> ***it is against unseen enemy forces.***

When we accuse and fight against one another we are actually helping the enemy out. It is not us against another person; it is all of us against the devil! All people are of immeasurable value to God.

"If you are wise and understand God's ways, prove it by living an honorable life, doing good works with the humility that comes from wisdom. But if you are bitterly jealous and there is selfish ambition in your heart, do not cover up the truth with boasting and lying. For jealousy and selfishness are not God's kind of wisdom. Such things are earthly, unspiritual, and demonic. For wherever there is jealousy and selfish ambition (whenever you are trying to look better than others and get the better of others), there you will find disorder and evil of every kind" (James 3:13-16 NLT).

God's Word says where there is contention and selfishness, that every evil thing and confusion is present and there are no mighty miracles done in that place.

When your mind automatically assumes that what was done was meant for ill intent, you need to arrest it and choose to believe the best about that situation.

So envision the best possible scenario and put your self in that person's shoes. This is what God would do. The God inside of you would act in love, and love believes the best of every person. The opposite is not God. Satan is the accuser of the brethren. So I want you to practice turning every scenario around and believing the best in it!

You say, "What about discernment, though? Should I not be able to discern who a person is?" Yes, you should, but should that change the way you act toward them and treat them? They are of immeasurable value to God just like you are. I am sure Jesus discerned Judas yet He washed his feet along with the other disciples. I am sure He discerned the woman who poured out the perfume on His feet and who she was, yet He allowed her to touch Him.

You cannot control what others do, so do not think about who else needs to hear this, the only change we can make is within ourselves.

We cannot control what others do, we can only control ourselves. One day each of us will stand before a Holy God, alone. There will not be anyone by our side to blame. Adam and Eve tried the blame game in the garden and both still had to face the consequences of their own actions.

Focus on you and looking in your own mirror. Matthew 7:3-5 says: "Deal with the plank in your eye and not the speck in your neighbors eye."

You can change the world - at least *your* world - by changing you. Believe the best of everyone and honor even those who despitefully use you. MIGHTY MIRACLES HAPPEN HERE!

"So this is my prayer: that your love will flourish and that you will not only love much but well. Live a lover's life, circumspect and exemplary, a life Jesus will be proud of: bountiful in fruits from the soul, making Jesus Christ attractive to all, getting everyone involved in the glory and praise of God" (Philippians 1:9-11 MSG).

Matthew 25:40 (ESV)
"And the King will answer them,
'Truly, I say to you, as you did
it to one of the least of these my
brothers, you did it to me.'"

2 Peter 3:9 (NIV)
"The Lord is not slow in keeping
his promise, as some understand
slowness. Instead he is patient, not
wanting anyone to perish."

John 3:16 (ESV)
"For God so loved the world, that
he gave his only Son, that whoever
believes in him should not perish
but have eternal life."

Matthew 10:31 (ESV)
"Fear not, therefore; you are of
more value than many sparrows."

Romans 8:32 (ESV)
"He who did not spare his own Son
but gave him up for us all."

Isaiah 43:4 (AMP)
"you are precious in My sight and
I love you."

Matthew 5:43-45 (KJV)
"Ye have heard that it hath been
said, Thou shalt love thy neighbor,
and hate thine enemy. But I say
unto you, Love your enemies,
bless them that curse you, do good
to them that hate you, and pray for
them which despitefully use you,
and persecute you; That ye may be
the children of your Father which
is in heaven: for he maketh his sun
to rise on the evil and on the good,
and sendeth rain on the just and on
the unjust."

Chapter 6

FORGIVE

If you have been hurt by someone, ***forgive*** them.
Sometimes you have to do this as an act of faith. Forgive
quickly, because when a wound is allowed to fester,
infection can set in.

You do not forgive them because you ***feel*** like it; you will
never feel like it.

Forgiveness is a decision not a feeling.
You do it as an act of faith.

Anyone who has hurt you ***just forgive them***. Do it. Say it
out loud in your time of prayer, Lord, I choose to forgive
_____. Forgiving them does not mean you have
set yourself up for more hurt and you do not have to be
buddy-buddy with them. You can be nice, respectful and
kind without being a door mat.
Forgiving them cuts the anchor loose that you have on
that hurt. If you refuse to let it go you will stay anchored
to that past hurt until you do.

The word for–**give** is going to involve **giving**. It is going to cost you. You know you have really forgiven someone, when you can give to them. It is called **for**give (to give before). It helps to realize that forgiving them is for you; it makes you free. As long as you are not forgiving, you are giving that hurt control and permission to dictate your life and future. You are keeping yourself under that person's power and clearly they do not have your best in mind. Why would you want someone who does not have your best in mind to control your life? That pain will determine how you react and respond to people and circumstances you encounter. You have become a hurting person that will, in turn, hurt others.

I can choose to for-give, whether they are sorry or not; because I am doing it for me, my here and now and my future.

In our minds we say that we are just going to make them pay. We say, "I deserve revenge," but that is not actually what is happening. We are only continuing to give them power to harm us. We are keeping the pain fresh and current each new day that we hold on to it and we do not deserve that. Focusing on it and talking about it is like reopening the wound over and over. A wound that is reopened cannot begin to heal until you stop reopening it.

Stop trying to get even with people who have hurt you. What you sow is what you will reap.

But God, that is not what I want to do. I want to ruin these people. They are wrong, and they know they are wrong. No, No, No! Those actions are just to protect my own feelings. James 3:14-16 says it is **pride, selfish, unwise, carnal** and every evil thing is present there.

62

1 Corinthians 3:3 says, "For you are still carnal. For where there are envy, strife, and divisions among you, are you not carnal and behaving like mere men?"

Galatians 5:15 says, "But if you bite and devour one another [in partisan strife], be careful that you [and your whole fellowship] are not consumed by one another."

In some of the things that happen in our lives, maybe God cannot get involved because we choose to handle it our own way.

Every time I step in His place of responsibility, He will not interfere. If I decide to get someone back because of my emotions, God figures, "Okay you have decided to handle this yourself, you do not need Me."

When you overcome evil with good, you may have to go through some stuff that is not comfortable; but you can believe, *well the Lord is going to handle that*. He does! While it may be wrong, if you believe the Lord is going to handle it, you leave God ***no other choice*** but to step into the spot you reserve for Him to show up in your life.

Look at the examples in the Bible where God showed up to deal with situations for people. Look at what they did vs. those who decided they wanted to handle it by themselves and God did not do anything. (Examples: Adam in the garden, Cain with the wrong sacrifice, Sarah & Abraham with the promise to be a father, and Samson having confidence in his own way and his own strength.)

Choose to do it God's way. Forgive quickly, for your own

good, and let Him handle it.

Are you not glad Jesus chose to forgive you while you were not deserving of it?

In Matthew 18:21-35 is the Parable of the Unforgiving Debtor:

"Then Peter came to him and asked, 'Lord, how often should I forgive someone who sins against me? Seven times?' 'No, not seven times,' Jesus replied, 'but seventy times seven! Therefore, the Kingdom of Heaven can be compared to a king who decided to bring his accounts up to date with servants who had borrowed money from him. In the process, one of his debtors was brought in who owed him millions of dollars. He could not pay, so his master ordered that he be sold—along with his wife, his children, and everything he owned—to pay the debt. But the man fell down before his master and begged him, "Please, be patient with me, and I will pay it all." Then his master was filled with pity for him, and he released him and forgave his debt. But when the man left the king, he went to a fellow servant who owed him a few thousand dollars. He grabbed him by the throat and demanded instant payment. His fellow servant fell down before him and begged for a little more time. "Be patient with me, and I will pay it," he pleaded. But his creditor would not wait. He had the man arrested and put in prison until the debt could be paid in full. When some of the other servants saw this, they were very upset. They went to the king and told him everything that had happened. Then the king called in the man he had forgiven and said, "You evil servant! I forgave you that tremendous debt because you pleaded with me.

Should not you have mercy on your fellow servant, just as I had mercy on you?" Then the angry king sent the man to prison to be tortured until he had paid his entire debt. That is what my heavenly Father will do to you if you refuse to forgive your brothers and sisters from your heart.'"

Romans 5:8 says, "But God showed his great love for us by sending Christ to die for us while we were still sinners."

To help you to forgive as an act of faith, take communion over it. Communion is a place where things are settled ("it is finished").

"Then He took a loaf [of bread], and when He had given thanks, He broke [it] and gave it to them saying, 'This is My body which is given for you; do this in remembrance of Me.' And in like manner, He took the cup after supper, saying, 'This cup is the new testament or covenant [ratified] in My blood, which is shed (poured out) for you'" (Luke 22:19-20 AMP).

Just as Christ forgave us, even while we were still sinners and He chose to love us, we are expected to forgive those who sin against us. When we break bread and drink the cup in communion, we are remembering all that we have been forgiven and how powerful that forgiveness is; so we, too, can forgive.

Having gratitude will change your attitude.

We are remembering the lashes that He took; His Word says, "By His stripes you were healed" (physically and emotionally). Not forgiving is a sin that keeps us bound to the hurts, but we are remembering in communion that sin has no power over us.

"He himself bore our sins" in His body on the cross, so **that we might die to sin** and live for righteousness; "by His wounds you have been healed" (1 Peter 2:24 NIV). As He laid His life down, He saw you. He saw your sin, your hurts, your pain and He sacrificed His life to be tortured. He endured it all knowing He was doing it to make you accepted and free.

Really every personal choice you make to be healed and have no more hurt is good; but there is nothing greater than the power of God that breaks every yoke of bondage and heals the broken hearted. Communion is recognizing you are not alone. You have the power of God working in and through you.

Nothing, no thing is greater than the power of God working in you. The power of God is surpassing of anything on the earth, under the earth or above the earth.

That is right, surpassing. That is like in a race where a runner speeds by all the others, like a flash. God's power surpasses any hurt or offense. Nothing is too big or too strong or too deep for God, nothing. He surpasses it all.

As you take communion, do it with remembrance of the power of God that will make you free of hurt. After you are free of the hurt, leave it there and do not pick it up again. Simply say, "No, that thing is nailed to the cross and buried with sin. I have risen up free of that and I am

66

free indeed. The power of God is stronger than anything."

I am reminded of the old song: "There is power, power, wonderworking power in the precious blood of the Lamb."

<u>The power of God is the answer you need.</u> All the rest of this book is good information but the power of God is what will transform you. Take communion as often as you can, even daily in remembrance of all God has done. Communion will help you to forgive and be able to declare "it is finished" over your hurts and offenses. It will release the power of God in your life.

Matthew 6:14-15 (NIV)
"For if you forgive men when they sin against you, your heavenly Father will also forgive you. But if you do not forgive men their sins, your Father will not forgive your sins."

2 Corinthians 5:21 (NLT)
"For God made Christ, who never sinned, to be the offering for our sin, so that we could be made right with God through Christ."

Luke 6:37 (AMP)
"Acquit, forgive and release (give up resentment, let it drop)."

Colossians 3:13 (NIV)
"Bear with each other and forgive one another if any of you has a grievance against someone. Forgive as the Lord forgave you."

Ephesians 4:31-32 (NIV)
"Get rid of all bitterness, rage and anger, brawling and slander, along with every form of malice. Be kind and compassionate to one another, forgiving each other, just as in Christ God forgave you."

John 8:7 (NIV)
"When they kept on questioning him, he straightened up and said to them, 'If any one of you is without sin, let him be the first to throw a stone at her.'"

1 John 4:8 (NKJV)
"He who does not love does not know God, for God is love."

John 13:35 (NKJV)
"By this all will know that you are My disciples, if you have love for one another."

Isaiah 40:27-31 (MSG)
"Haven't you been listening? GOD doesn't come and go. God lasts. He's Creator of all you can see or imagine. He doesn't get tired out, doesn't pause to catch his breath. And he knows everything, inside and out. He energizes those who get tired, gives fresh strength to dropouts. For even young people tire and drop out, young folk in their prime stumble and fall. But those who wait upon GOD get fresh strength. They spread their wings and soar like eagles, They run and don't get tired, they walk and don't lag behind."

Chapter 7

Stop Reliving it

When you re-live a hurt, you nourish it. What the devil loves to do is get you hurt or offended by someone or something and then keep bringing it up so you get stuck focusing on it.

God's Word says: Yesterday is gone and today is brand new.

2 Corinthians 5:17 (NKJV) says, "Therefore, if anyone is in Christ, he is a new creation; old things have passed away; behold, all things have become new."

Do not nourish the hurt. Think on these things: whatsoever things are lovely and of good report. Nourish the Word and starve the thoughts that dwell on the hurt.

Philippians 4:8 (AMP) says, "Finally, believers, whatever is true, whatever is honorable and worthy of respect, whatever is right and confirmed by God's word, whatever is pure and wholesome, whatever is lovely and brings peace, whatever is admirable and of good repute; if there is any excellence, if there is anything worthy of praise,

<u>think continually on these things [center your mind on them, and implant them in your heart].</u>"

It is so serious to let hurt feelings go because 5 years or 20 years is too long to be reliving it. When we keep reliving it and retelling it, it is as if we are ripping the scab off the wound each time. This only keeps it from healing. Forgiveness is like putting armor on that will keep any hurt from being able to get in.

"Above all, take up the shield of faith with which you will be able to quench **all** the fiery darts of the wicked one" (Ephesians 6:16 NKJV).

Hurt is like a spear. All it wants to do is cause and inflict more wounds. You **_must_** release everyone who has hurt you. You **_must_** release every wrong that has been done to you. You may think, *but my heart is hard*; you cannot even hear from God. You may think, *I am hurt so I cannot trust anyone anymore*: how will you be able to trust God?

Luke 10:19 says, "'Behold, I give you the authority to trample on serpents and scorpions, and over all the power of the enemy, and nothing shall by any means hurt you.'"

Matthew 6:26-28 (NKJV) says, "'Look at the birds of the air, for they neither sow nor reap nor gather into barns; yet your heavenly Father feeds them. Are you not of more value than they? Which of you by worrying can add one cubit to his stature? So why do you worry about clothing? Consider the lilies of the field, how they grow: they neither toil nor spin.'"

When we say, "but you do not understand this thing is 'real'", it is like you are saying He's not. As if the Bible is not for "real" life.

Paul figured this out in Philippians 3:12-14: "Not that I have already attained, or am already perfected; but I press on, that I may lay hold of that for which Christ Jesus has also laid hold of me. Brethren, I do not count myself to have apprehended; but one thing I do, forgetting those things which are behind and reaching forward to those things which are ahead, I press toward the goal for the prize of the upward call of God in Christ Jesus."

By holding on to our past or by retelling it, we are allowing our past to dictate, to be the focus of our future. *I do not want that thing to be calling forth my future!* Your hurt is trying to keep you looking behind.

Paul is saying: "take my word for it, you forget the past by reaching forward." The word <u>press</u> means that there is opposition, or something coming against. You have to <u>press</u> on. He is saying, "in all my getting of knowledge, this one thing I do:

I forget those things which are behind by reaching forward."

We are so focused on the past, not the future. We are focused on that thing that happened or what they said. That rejection. That abandonment. That loss. That mistake.

The reason we are so hurt is because we have a hook on that thing in the past. We are focused on the hurt, we are nourishing that hurt. We are looking back. Runners in a race do not look back because it slows them down and can even cause them to trip and fall. When you are looking back, you tend to dwell in a place of hurt, regret and disappointment. We think and talk about the things we missed out on; what we should have done different. We cannot change the past but we **can** press on.

We reap what we sow. If we spend time thinking on the hurt, we are sowing those seeds of hurt in our current life. Get a visual of that right now: see yourself standing there scattering hurt seeds into the garden of your life. When you plant seeds of hurt, you will have a crop of hurt coming. Stop the crop of hurt from coming by stopping the planting of more hurt seeds. Get in there and rip up any seeds that are planted and get to planting good seeds that will produce a crop you want to live with. Thinking on the evil that has been done to us will only produce more evil.

You do not change a mistake by continuing to make mistakes. We have to let go of the hurt and press on. Overcome evil with good.

Get ready because someone is going to bring it up to you!

Remember the word **press** means that there will be opposition. The enemy is like a fighter; he comes in and keeps trying to hit you in the same spot to wound you.

He is going to hit you in the spot that hurt you yesterday.

He plays dirty, like we see in football sometimes. If there is a player with a knee injury, you will see the other team trying to hit him in that knee so they can get him out of the game for good.

We have got to get in and **press on**. One thing God told me to do when I have been through the ringer is to **dress my best**, no matter how I feel. (Matthew 6:16-18)

You see, you have got to confuse hell. They cannot see or know that they are getting to you with those constant jabs. If you laugh at famine and disaster, you have got the enemy of your soul saying, "Wait a minute. Did I not just hit them there? I do not understand. Why are they still smiling? They should be rocking in a corner!" This throws the enemy off and he will not keep hitting that spot, if it will not hurt you.

Once you forgive, stop re-living it over and over.
You have got to let it go.

Stop wearing your feelings on your sleeve. You know people everyone knows they are hurt and something is wrong? Do not do that. We are to be wearing the garments of praise. Dress up in the joy of the Lord. Get to church early and actually participate with praise service. Great deliverance can come in a praise service.

When we dwell on the hurt, we are sowing seeds to that hurt and seeds of hurt reap a harvest of hurt. Whatever you focus on is the target you will hit.

Do you catch yourself reliving it saying, *"if only…"* ? At the time of salvation you have a new name, a new heritage and a new blood line. The past has been washed away. You are made brand new. *Generational curses are broken*. You are no longer of that blood line. Praise the Lord. So why continue to relive it?

Just be the difference you desire to see in the world. We can get all hurt and upset at why there is no love or joy or peace in the world. Yet, when we do, we are a part of the problem and not the solution. We are the hurt people, hurting people. Someone's got to step up and just be the difference. If you want the world to be a better place, it starts with you. You be the difference you desire to see, and while you are changing your own world, you will be changing the world at large.

Isaiah 43   MSG

"Forget about what's
happened;
don't keep going over old
history,"

pastorrhondaj Today is a brand new day, with new opportunities, new potential and new possibilities. Yesterday is GONE, so forget about it! Today has a brand new 24 for you to make something great out of!

Isaiah 43:18 (AMP)
"Do not remember the former things, or ponder the things of the past."

Phil 4:4-9 (AMP)
"Rejoice in the Lord always [delight, take pleasure in Him]; again I will say, rejoice! Let your gentle spirit [your graciousness, unselfishness, mercy, tolerance, and patience] be known to all people. The Lord is near. Do not be anxious or worried about anything, but in everything [every circumstance and situation] by prayer and petition with thanksgiving, continue to make your [specific] requests known to God. And the peace of God [that peace which reassures the heart, that peace] which transcends all understanding, [that peace which] stands guard over your hearts and your minds in Christ Jesus [is yours].

Finally, believers, whatever is true, whatever is honorable and worthy of respect, whatever is right and confirmed by God's word, whatever is pure and wholesome, whatever is lovely and brings peace, whatever is admirable and of good repute; if there is any excellence, if there is anything worthy of praise, think continually on these things [center your mind on them, and implant them in your heart]. The things which you have learned and received and heard and seen in me, practice these things [in daily life], and the God [who is the source] of peace and well-being will be with you."

Chapter 8

I CANNOT FORGET

If I am supposed to "forget those things which are behind," why can't I?

I had a young woman come to me for prayer. She said: "I have forgiven but I just cannot forget. It will randomly come up in my mind over and over. I am stuck and I cannot shake this to move on. It is really affecting me. I so badly do not want this to keep holding me back." I prayed for her and went about my day. A few days later I woke up with a strong prophetic response from God for her. I intended to send it in a message to her, but I got busy and forgot. Then later that day, I was going down the church driveway (on a day I was not usually there) and God spoke it again. Okay God, as soon as I get inside I will send her a message. As I walked down the hall, I heard her voice coming from another Pastor's office (she is never at the church during the week). Now I was completely convinced this was the voice of God and it was very important that I share what God said with her.

"The fact that you remember has no affect on your current status. The devil would like you to think, because you remember, that it is affecting you and holding you back. In actuality, the memory is a reminder of your victory and <u>what you have already conquered.</u> It should cause you to raise your shoulders and lift your chin at every remembrance that comes."

Wow, how awesome. What the devil means for bad and to destroy us with, is the very thing that God uses to remind us of our victories.

In Joshua chapter 4 the Israelites crossed over the Jordan River (the river had parted open for them to walk across on dry ground). God told them to take stones **from the middle** of the Jordan. He told them to build a memorial with the stones *so they would remember* their victory and be able to tell their children about what God had done. So those memories from the middle of your painful places in the past; they are not there to destroy you. That is a lie from the enemy. They are there to remind you of what you have survived already and what you have been able to conquer. So go ahead and take those rocks (memories) from the middle of your pain and use them as a stepping stone; use them to elevate yourself to another level. You are stronger and better knowing what you have already been able to conquer.

I pondered on this for a while and asked God why He created us this way, to not be able to forget.

Again, God was faithful to respond:

"If you forgot, you would not have faith for tomorrow's mountains or valleys. Each time you face something new, if you had forgotten what you already made it through, you would need to start all over with brand new, baby faith."

The reason you do not forget is to build your faith. You will now know you can climb the highest mountain and that God **is** with you in the darkest valleys. This is how your faith is able to increase.

So the next time the devil brings up your past to condemn you, do not drop your chin and slump your shoulders. Lift your head and say, "**Yes and I survived** that, so I am better and stronger. That is a memorial of my faith in my powerful God! Is that not beautiful? That represents my faith. I do not want to forget because I want to know that my faith in God will take me through anything I will face in my future."

The forgetting we are supposed to do is:
-Forget about it in the manner that the devil would like to use it, to destroy you.
-Forget about it in the way that you think it is holding you back and keeping you from moving ahead.
-Forget about it in the way that it is so painful.
-**Do not forget as a reminder** of your victory and what you have already conquered.
-Do not forget **because it holds your faith to face tomorrow**.

Change the way you think about "forgetting those things

which are behind," *the way the devil would like you to think about it*. But do not forget the way God wants you to see it. God never intended the rocks the Israelites pulled from the middle of the Jordan to remind them of pain, fear and suffering. That would be sick and twisted and that is what the devil tries to do to us. He tries to twist our thinking so we see those memories as painful; **the pain is what we are supposed to forget.** It says in Revelation 12:11 we overcome "by the blood of the Lamb and the word of our testimony". So testify of the victories in your past so your future knows <u>**you have no fear, only stronger faith**</u>.

Romans 5:3 (NLT)
"We can rejoice, too, when we run into problems and trials, for we know that they help us develop endurance."

Genesis 50:20 (KJV)
"But as for you, ye thought evil against me; but God meant it unto good, to bring to pass, as it is this day, to save much people alive."

Isaiah 43:1-2, 5 (AMP)
"Fear not, for I have redeemed you [ransomed you by paying a price instead of leaving you captives]; I have called you by your name; you are Mine. When you pass through the waters, I will be with you, and through the rivers, they will not overwhelm you. When you walk through the fire, you will not be burned or scorched, nor will the flame kindle upon you.
Fear not, for I am with you."

Revelation 12:11 (NLT)
"And they have defeated him by the blood of the Lamb and by their testimony."

Romans 8:37 (NLT)
"No, despite all these things, overwhelming victory is ours through Christ, who loved us."

Philippians 4:13 (BSB)
"I can do all things through Christ who gives me strength."

Colossians 1:10-12 (BSB)
"Walk in a manner worthy of the Lord and may please Him in every way: bearing fruit in every good work, growing in the knowledge of God, being strengthened with all power according to His glorious might so that you may have full endurance and patience, and joyfully giving thanks to the Father."

1 Corinthians 16:13 (NLT)
"Be on guard. Stand firm in the faith. Be courageous. Be strong."

Chapter 9

COMMUNICATE

I spent many years hurt and being the very cause of the pain I was carrying because of my communication skills. I felt like I was not being heard, like I was facing a brick wall, and I was. I had built that brick wall with my own words, negativity, ranting and nagging.

Much of our hurt can happen because of communication or the lack thereof.

How we have communicated and the tone of our communication can cause hurt on both sides. Feeling like you have no voice and you are not being heard can leave you hurt and you will continue to propel hurt. So let's take a look at communication.

First, if you have a problem with someone or think they have a problem with you, the Bible is very clear on how to handle this. Before I quote the scripture, let's look real quick at this "if you have a problem with someone or think they have a problem with you." How often do we communicate through complaints or negative statements? Many times our conversations can be full of negatives and complaining. No one wants to be around a "Debbie

Downer," yet that is exactly what we might be. Make sure your conversations have a balance of good over bad. If it is always a complaint or negative, as soon as the person sees you coming, your voice is already going to be shut off. If you want someone to want to listen to you, make sure the majority of your conversations with them are happy and up-lifting.

Make sure you have a proper balance of good and positive communication in order to be received.

I have good news for you! It is so easy to change that balance if people have perceived you to be negative in the past. You can change it by simply adding to the good and positive side of the balance today. Some say to use the sandwich method, which is you say something good and nice, then you squeeze the complaint in the middle and you end it with a good thing again. I would say take it a step further and, before you even have to communicate in a sandwich form, make sure your conversations are mostly good and positive. Then you will have more of a voice when you need to point out something that may not be so positive.

Okay, so, back to the Word of God on the matter of when you have ought with someone or you think they have ought with you. You are to go to that person privately.

Matthew 18:15-16 (NASB)
"'If your brother sins, go and show him his fault in private; if he listens to you, you have won your brother. But if he does not listen to you, take one or two more with you, so that <u>by the mouth of two or three witnesses every fact may be confirmed.</u>'"

82

Matthew 18:21-22 (NASB)

"Then Peter came and said to Him, 'Lord, how often shall my brother sin against me and I forgive him? Up to seven times?' Jesus said to him, 'I do not say to you, up to seven times, but up to seventy times seven.'"

Galatians 6:1 (NIV)

"Brothers and sisters, if someone is caught in a sin, you who live by the Spirit should restore that person gently. But watch yourselves, or you also may be tempted."

Titus 3:10 (NIV)

"Warn a divisive person once, and then warn them a second time. After that, have nothing to do with them."

We are to first go to that person, not call 3 friends or talk to a few people about it; that would be gossip. Gossip causes hurt in you and everyone you infect with it. We are to go to that person gently and wisely. The Word of God says in James 1:5 that if anyone lacks wisdom, ask and He will give it. If you need help with what to say, pray and ask God. He will give you the words to say.

Matthew 5:9 says: "Blessed are the peacemakers."

Our communication that leads us to hurt tends to be in the heat of the moment when we speak out. Our tone is harsh, our voice can be loud and our demeanor can be intense. Maybe you do not communicate this way, but instead, you keep a soft tone, you just lace it with sarcasm. I promise you, in this moment, nothing you say is being heard and you are only leading into more hurt. You are adding bricks and mortar to the wall that is being built. The other person has their defenses up and they are not listening to a thing you are saying. Venom is being spewed and hurt is being produced.

What we need to learn how to do is shut our mouths in moments that are intense, put the flame out and add no wood to it. God forbid we add gasoline to the fire and then sit back and feel bad at how hurt we are. You do not always have to speak or share your thoughts or opinion. If you want to be heard and have successful communication that does not add to the wall or the fire, you should hold your voice until a later time. Wait until things are good. Wait until you have prayed for wisdom and the right words to say, and then communicate. This way you can know you will be heard and your voice will have successful impact. Over food that you have made or prepared is always a good time to communicate. Food makes people feel good, and their defenses are not up.

Do not rant or nag. That is like a leaky faucet dripping and no one wants to listen to that (Proverbs 27:15). You will be left feeling hurt because you were not heard; but you were the one that produced that result. Sometimes you will just have to deal with things not being the way you want them to be; until you can communicate without gasoline or putting bricks and mortar on the wall. Nagging will not work, it will hurt you. When you are praying to God asking Him for the right words, ask for a word picture. A word picture is a way of getting someone to see your perspective by telling a story about a completely unrelated scenario that describes how you feel about the actual thing that is going on. Here is an example of a word picture: I was having an issue dealing with some situations where I felt things were being done sloppily and there was a lack of effort on someone's part at work. So, rather than nagging or ranting at my husband (the boss), I decided to choose my battles, to be patient, and to overlook what was frustrating me. I wanted to make sure I was heard, so I waited until things were good. I waited until I had prayed and got my word picture from God, then I communicated. I shared about an experience we both had with a baseball league our boys played on for a season. In this league, no one ever got a strike or got "out," there were no foul balls and no one kept score, everyone was a winner. Well, this was not getting any of those children ready for real life. It produced an attitude that they did not need to try hard, put any kind of effort in or work on their skills. I remembered that time and that my husband agreed with me. I was then able to say, this is how I feel about the other situation. This was successful communication. There was no nagging, no ranting, no gasoline, no bricks and mortar, and I was heard. I was able to leave the conversation with no hurt and feeling valued.

Here is a passage from the Bible where God sent a prophet to use a word picture with the king. "So the Lord sent Nathan the prophet to tell David this story: 'There were two men in a certain town. One was rich, and one was poor. The rich man owned a great many sheep and cattle. The poor man owned nothing but one little lamb he had bought. He raised that little lamb, and it grew up with his children. It ate from the man's own plate and drank from his cup. He cuddled it in his arms like a baby daughter. One day a guest arrived at the home of the rich man. But instead of killing an animal from his own flock or herd, he took the poor man's lamb and killed it and prepared it for his guest.' David was furious. 'As surely as the Lord lives,' he vowed, 'any man who would do such a thing deserves to die! He must repay four lambs to the poor man for the one he stole and for having no pity.' Then Nathan said to David, 'You are that man! The Lord, the God of Israel, says: "I anointed you king of Israel and saved you from the power of Saul. I gave you your master's house and his wives and the kingdoms of Israel and Judah. And if that had not been enough, I would have given you much, much more. Why, then, have you despised the word of the Lord and done this horrible deed? For you have murdered Uriah the Hittite with the sword of the Ammonites and stolen his wife"' (2 Samuel 12:1-9 NLT). King David saw how wrong he had been and repented. Pray for wisdom and the right words to say and God will give you a word picture to help communicate your perspective.

Word pictures are a powerful communication tool used even in the Word of God.

Make sure you pay attention to your non-verbal communication - your body language. Sit level with them, do not stand over them. Make sure you are smiling and not scowling. Do not cross your legs or arms. Lean in. Be aware of your tone, keep it gentle.

Here is another way I have learned to communicate with my husband. Because we can nag and rant, they are often on the defensive. If they know we are bothered, they are going to try to fix it, or try to fix us and this tends to lead to fights. They are fixers, that is what they do. They think, when we are communicating something that is bothering us, that we are imploring them to do something about it. So what I have learned is to let him off the hook first by saying, "Please do not fix this. Actually, I do not even really need you to respond. As a woman, I just have a need to talk to someone and feel like I am being heard. I am not asking you to fix anything or say anything."

When we communicate to "win" or "be right" we lose.

If you are communicating to "win" it could be a fight to the death, at least the death of the relationship. If you are fighting to "be right" it will result in hurt feelings, things said that you did not really mean, spewing, and a draw because both people (in their own perspective) are "right." Proverbs 21:2 says, "Every man's way is right in his own eyes." I remember the freedom I experienced when I first learned this. I was able to look at my husband when we started down the path of a disagreement or in the heat of one and say "okay, you are right." Hahahaha! The look on his face the first time I conceded was priceless. I was serious too. I had come to the realization that, in our own minds, we were both convinced we were 100% right and that is just the way we each saw things. So, he was right. I just told myself, "It is okay, I know I am right, but this is not worth the hurt that it will cause." Two people can look at the same thing and see something completely different. This does not make them bad or wrong, just normal. Everyone sees things differently through their own lens and everyone is right in their own eyes. Stop fighting to be "right" it will just end in hurt.

Maybe you do not get intense and you do not lace your conversation with sarcasm, but you are the silent type that just bottles it up. The Word of God tells us to go to that person. We are to communicate. Holding it in will only cause bitterness and hurt. Do communicate. Sometimes we are hurt because we do not communicate.

For whatever reason or excuse, we do not think we can or should.

**We should communicate; just in the right timing,
the right tone, be willing to concede
and maybe overlook some things.**

You never have to leave a conversation feeling hurt again.

James 3 teaches us to tame the tongue, that it is like a bit in a horse's mouth or a rudder on a ship: with just a little bit of pressure, you can change the course you are on. Even though the winds can be strong, a little pressure on the rudder of a huge ship can change its direction. If you put a little bit of pressure on your tongue to make good communication, you can change the direction a relationship or conversation is going. So put a little pressure on your tongue, maybe to hold your voice, to not respond in the heat of the moment, or to overlook what is bothering you until you have prayed and you get God's wisdom and His words to say. Put a little pressure on your tongue not to get intense. Put a little pressure on your tongue not to fight to be right. Put a little pressure on your tongue to not keep repeating what is bothering you. A little pressure can change the direction of the conversation and the relationship.

You will find that you are being heard and that your voice will be powerful and effective. The choice is yours and the power is in your tongue.

James 3:8-9 (NASB)
"But no one can tame the tongue; it is a restless evil and full of deadly poison. With it we bless our Lord and Father, and with it we curse men, who have been made in the likeness of God."

James 1:19-20 (NKJV)
Qualities Needed in Trials
"So then, my beloved brethren, let every man be swift to hear, slow to speak, slow to wrath; for the wrath of man does not produce the righteousness of God."

Proverbs 12:25 (ESV)
"Anxiety in a man's heart weighs him down, but a good word makes him glad."

Proverbs 25:11 (ESV)
"A word fitly spoken is like apples of gold in a setting of silver."

Matthew 12:37 (ESV)
"'For by your words you will be justified, and by your words you will be condemned.'"

Ephesians 4:29 (ESV)
"Let no corrupting talk come out of your mouths, but only such as is good for building up, as fit's the occasion, that it may give grace to those who hear it."

Chapter 10

Healed. NO MORE HURT

I can truly say that NO THING can hurt me. I was talking to a friend about a family member that is elderly and slipping in her mind. She has reverted back to a time of great pain in her life that was abusive and hurtful. It is so sad seeing her reliving that hurt today. It was in that moment, though, that I realized *that will never be me.* First of all, I have the mind of Christ and a sound mind. But also, those things that were meant to hurt me have no effect on me. They are not buried or suppressed, they are gone. You can poke the wounds and scars all day and it does not hurt me anymore.

About a month after this conversation with my friend, I got put to the test! I had one of the biggest wounds of my past poked. We had over $40,000 stolen from us by a couple we had invested it with. I walked through that valley asking God to help me and putting all these principles He had taught me into practice, daily (some days, moment by moment). I came through better than before and God restored the money and beyond in different ways. I truly believed I had no more hurt over that.

I was walking down a hallway at a meeting I was attending and came around the corner to be face to face with that friend who squealed with delight to see me again. It had been years. I invited her into my meeting and introduced my friend to the others who were in attendance. About 45 minutes into the meeting, with my friend sitting next to me, I heard a still small voice in my mind say: "This is the woman who stole all that money from you" (I knew this, I knew her well. I knew her way back from high school). I was so excited I wanted to shout from the rooftops, I am healed, I am free, I have no more hurt. I could barely contain my excitement. It was like getting an A+ on a big test that I had studied so hard for. I did not recognize the pain or hurt from that, it took me 45 minutes to acknowledge it and even then I only felt compassion and empathy for her. I was free.

Nothing has the ability in my life to hurt me, by any means, and nothing has the ability in your life to hurt you, by any means.

Proverbs 1

33 But all who listen to me will live in peace, untroubled by fear of harm.

I pray that through my journey and the testimonies in this book you will be able to rejoice at passing the test, and live a life with no more hurt.

You can learn to have no more hurt in your life. Actually, God desires that nothing would hurt you. This does not happen overnight; it comes from lifelong, daily, moment by moment choices to act on scripture and not on our own protective feelings.

It will not be easy to change yourself. If you truly want to live free of hurt like you say you do, you must be committed to doing the following:

1. Know you have been given authority over all the power of the enemy. Luke 10:19 says, "'Behold, I give you the authority over all the power of the enemy, and nothing shall by any means hurt you."

2. Pay attention to your own reactions to people and situations. Ask yourself, "What am I feeling, and why am I feeling this way?" Listen to yourself. What is the conversation going on in your mind? Does it sound like "the peace of God" type of talk? Or is it more along the lines of defensiveness and frustration? Once you have identified the thinking that is exalting itself above the way that God would have you think, simply refuse to listen to those wrong ways of thinking. We must hold what God says about us above, as more valuable and important than, what anyone else says or does. If we are believing what other people say as truth and valuing it, we are making them above God. When you know your worth and value comes from God and how much He loves you, it will cast out all fear and nothing anyone else says or does can affect

you. You will be solid and immovable.

3. Remind yourself that you are accepted by the One who matters most. You have been adopted into the family of God.

4. Stop the cycle of hurting people hurt people by keeping the cycle of love going. Every time you love, you open yourself up to be vulnerable; every time you become vulnerable, it is inevitable you will get hurt; every time you get hurt, you must choose to forgive and then love again.

5. It is not all about you. Other people, like you, have immeasurable value to God. Honor everyone; even your enemies.

6. Make yourself free of the hurt by forgiving them, even if they do not deserve it or ask for it. You do deserve it (freedom from hurt).

7. Stop reliving it. Replace these wrong ways of thinking with the scriptures concerning God's ways of processing hurt and offense. Forget about the past and press on. Only keep the memory as a reminder of your victory.

8. Practice being heard. Communicate effectively, sandwich your words and make sure the positive communication far outweighs the negative.

9. Read the Word of God daily. Get the truth in you. Act out the instructions of the scriptures. Do what the Word says! Refuse to do things the way you have in the past! Only then will you find maturity happening in your life, and only then will you be on the preventative side of hurt!

There is a day coming when you will be able to say:

"I am healed, I have no more hurt."

Press on toward the mark. What you aim at is the target you will hit.

Ecclesiastes 7:20-22 (NKJV)
"For there is not a just man on earth who does good and does not sin. Also do not take to heart everything people say, lest you hear your servant cursing you. For many times, also, your own heart has known that even you have cursed others."

Mark 6:3-5 (NKJV)
"'Is this not the carpenter, the Son of Mary, and brother of James, Joses, Judas, and Simon? And are not His sisters here with us?' So they were offended at Him. But Jesus said to them, 'A prophet is not without honor except in his own country,
among his own relatives, and in his own house.' Now He could do no mighty work there, except that He laid His hands on a few sick people and healed them."

Mark 4:16-17 (AMP)
"'And in the same way the ones sown upon stony ground are those who, when they hear the Word, at once receive and accept and welcome it with joy; and they have no real root in themselves, and so they endure for a little while; then when trouble or persecution arises on account of the Word, they immediately are offended (become displeased, indignant, resentful) and they stumble and fall away.'"

Matthew 24:10-13 (AMP)
"'And then many will be offended and repelled and will begin to distrust and desert [Him Whom they ought to trust and obey] and will stumble and fall away and betray one another and pursue one another with hatred. And many false prophets will rise up and deceive and lead many into error. And the love of the great body of people will grow cold because of the multiplied lawlessness and iniquity, but he who endures to the end will be saved.'"

1 Corinthians 13:5 (AMP)
"Love (God's love in us) does not insist on it's own rights or it's own way, for it is not self-seeking; it is not touchy or fretful or resentful; it takes no account of the evil done to it [it pays no attention to a suffered wrong]."

Romans 12:2 (NIV)
"Do not conform any longer to the pattern of this world, but be transformed by the renewing of your mind. Then you will be able to test and approve what God's will is - his good, pleasing and perfect will."

2 Corinthians 2:11 (NKJV) *advises us to be aware of this danger.*
"Lest Satan should take advantage of us; for we are not ignorant of his devices."

94

2 Corinthians 10:3-5 (NKJV)
***Provides directions on how to
renew our minds:***
"For though we walk in the flesh,
we do not war after the flesh: (For
the weapons of our warfare are not
carnal, but mighty through God to
the pulling down of strong holds;)
Casting down imaginations, and
every high thing that exalteth
itself against the knowledge of
God, and bringing into captivity
every thought to the obedience of
Christ."

Philippians 1:9-10 (KJV)
"And this I pray, that your love
may abound yet more and more
in knowledge and in all judgment;
That ye may approve things that
are excellent; that ye may be
sincere and without offense till the
day of Christ"

Ephesians 4:27 (AMP)
"Leave no [such] room or foothold
for the devil [give no opportunity
to him]."

Proverbs 4:23 (NLT)
"Guard your heart above all else,
for it determines the course of your
life."
Psalm 119:101 (NASB)
"I have restrained my feet from
every evil way, That I may keep
Your word."

Proverbs 22:3 (AMP)
"A prudent man foresees evil and
hides himself, But the simple pass
on and are punished."

1 Peter 5:8 (NKJV)
"Be sober, be vigilant; because
your adversary the devil walks
about like a roaring lion, seeking
whom he may devour."

2 Timothy 4:5 (NKJV)
"But you be watchful in all
things…"

Deuteronomy 4:9 (NKJV)
"Only take heed to yourself, and
diligently keep yourself, lest you
forget the things your eyes have
seen, and lest they depart from
your heart all the days of your life.
And teach them to your children
and your grandchildren."

Psalm 18:33 (AMP)
"He makes my feet like hinds'
feet [able to stand firmly or make
progress on the dangerous heights
of testing and trouble]; He sets me
securely upon my high places."

Acts 14:22 (AMP)
"Establishing and strengthening
the souls and the hearts of the
disciples, urging and warning and
encouraging them to stand firm in
the faith, and [telling them] that
it is through many hardships and
tribulations we must enter the
kingdom of God."

1 Corinthians 10:12-13 (AMP)
"Therefore let anyone who thinks
he stands [who feels sure that
he has a steadfast mind and is
standing firm], take heed lest he
fall [into sin]. For no temptation
(no trial regarded as enticing to
sin), [no matter how it comes
or where it leads] has overtaken
you and laid hold on you that is
not common to man [that is, no
temptation or trial has come to you
that is beyond human resistance
and that is not adjusted and
adapted and belonging to human
experience, and such as man can
bear]. But God is faithful [to His
Word and to His compassionate
nature], and He [can be trusted] not

to let you be tempted and tried and assayed beyond your ability and strength of resistance and power to endure, but with the temptation He will [always] also provide the way out (the means of escape to [c] a landing place), that you may be capable and strong and powerful to bear up under it patiently."

Proverbs 12:18 (NKJV)
"There is one who speaks like the piercings of a sword, But the tongue of the wise promotes health."

Psalm 147:3 (ESV)
"He heals the brokenhearted And binds up their wounds."

Proverbs 18:14 (NKJV)
"The spirit of a man will sustain him in sickness, But who can bear a broken spirit?"
(If you are strong in spirit it will sustain you)

James 4:7 (AMP)
"So be subject to God. Resist the devil [stand firm against him], and he will flee from you."

66445061R00063

Made in the USA
Charleston, SC
20 January 2017